SUN CITY

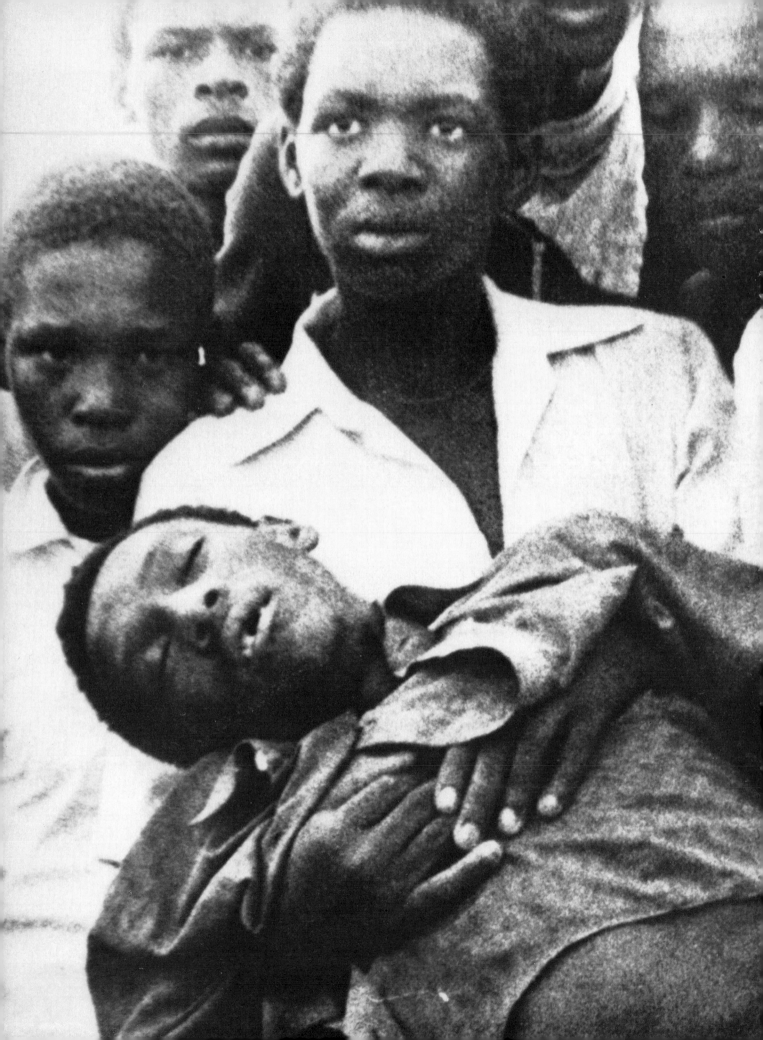

To the memory of

VUYISILE MINI

Trade union activist,
musician, and composer
of Freedom Songs

In November 1964,
he and his codefendants
went to the gallows
in South Africa,
singing his songs.

and

To all those who have died
for the freedom
of South Africa

(Left) A young man, injured when the police opened fire on a crowd of mourners attending a funeral, is carried away by his friends. *(Photo: Reuters/Bettman Newsphotos)*

Video photos by Cathe Ishino.

SUN CITY

BY ARTISTS UNITED AGAINST APARTHEID

THE STRUGGLE FOR FREEDOM IN SOUTH AFRICA

THE MAKING OF
THE RECORD
BY DAVE MARSH

PENGUIN BOOKS
Viking Penguin Inc., 40 West 23rd Street,
New York, New York 10010, U.S.A.
Penguin Books Ltd, Harmondsworth,
Middlesex, England
Penguin Books Australia Ltd, Ringwood,
Victoria, Australia
Penguin Books Canada Limited, 2801 John Street,
Markham, Ontario, Canada L3R 1B4
Penguin Books (N.Z.) Ltd, 182–190 Wairau Road,
Auckland 10, New Zealand

First published in Penguin Books 1985
Published simultaneously in Canada

Produced by Cloverdale Press,
133 Fifth Avenue,
New York, New York 10003

Grateful acknowledgment is made for permission to reprint excerpts
from the followng publications:

South Africa Information Packet by the Washington Office on Africa
Educational Fund. Reprinted by permission

The Apartheid Handbook by Roger Omond. Copyright © Roger
Omond, 1985. Reprinted by permission of Penguin Books Ltd.

117 Days by Ruth First. Reprinted by permission of the Estate of Ruth
First.

Typography by *Paragraphics,* New York, New York

Printed in the United States of America by Command Web Offset Inc.,
Secaucus, New Jersey

"**Apartheid** (pronounced *apart-hate*) is a word meaning 'apart' or 'separate.' It is the system of legalized racism in the Republic of South Africa. Under apartheid, all persons in South Africa are classified by the color of their skin into the following races: African; White (persons of European descent); Colored (persons of racially mixed descent); and Asian (mostly persons of Indian descent). Although there are only 4.5 million whites, under the repressive system of apartheid, they control every aspect of life for the 24 million blacks (including Africans, Coloreds, and Asians)."

The Washington Office on Africa Educational Fund

In May 1985, as unrest dramatically increased, South African police armed with semiautomatic rifles were seen for the first time in the Johannesburg city centre. *(Photo: Reuters/Bettman Newsphotos)*

The anti-apartheid rally at the Citicorp Center. *(Photo: Reuven Kopitchinski)*

Little Steven and Lou Reed. *(Photo: Chase Roe)*

PREFACE

The song "Sun City" was born out of outrage and the desire to educate. The thrust of this effort has been to stimulate awareness, to ask all people everywhere to get involved by singing along and informing themselves about South Africa. Our hope is also that, once informed, we all might take a closer look at our own consciences and the disease of racism in our own culture.

This being our intention, we were overjoyed when Alan Kellock, the president and publisher of Viking-Penguin, approached us with the idea of a book about the "Sun City" project and the issue that inspired it. Jeff Weiss and the staff at Cloverdale Press said they could bring it together, and they have.

This book was finished so quickly because a number of friends agreed to donate their efforts. Danny Schechter suggested the book project and helped produce it. Dave Marsh sat down with us and wrote a text on the making of the record, which summarized the four months of dedication, commitment, and hard work of dozens of people, including over fifty artists. Rick Dutka, a member of the "Sun City" record project provided invaluable help. And special thanks to Chris Kinser and Barbara Becker of Cloverdale Press for editorial wizardry, and to Paul Matarazzo and J.C. Suares for art direction. David Seelig of Star File and other committed photographers made pictures available. Writer Bill Adler contributed the artist bios. Zöe Yanakis was coordinator extraordinaire. Friends at anti-apartheid groups shared their work as well. The information presented comes from various sources, notably the publications of The Africa Fund, the Washington Office on Africa, Donald Woods and the Lincoln Trust, International Defence and Aid, and the United Nations Centre Against Apartheid.

In this book, you will find photographs of the "Sun City" sessions, comments by the artists involved, and the lyrics to the songs. There's the inside story of how the record and the video came together. It's the story of what we did, how we did it, and why we did it. And we are hopeful that it will inspire others to tackle similar projects.

This is not a "rock book" in any traditional sense. If anything, we view it more as a *rock* of the kind David hurled at Goliath—a compendium of the type of information that moves people of conscience to become involved, to act. We want it to be useful and hope it reaches readers unfamiliar with the vast literature on apartheid. Perhaps it will stimulate readers to seek out more comprehensive sources of information.

The royalties from this book, as well as from the record, are being donated to The Africa Fund, a nonprofit charitable trust registered with the United Nations. The money will support political prisoners and their families inside South Africa, the educational and cultural needs of exiles, and the educational efforts of anti-apartheid groups. Readers who want to contribute to these projects can send their own tax-deductible donations to:

The Africa Fund
198 Broadway
New York, New York 10038

The Africa Fund also publishes a list of organizations working against apartheid. Why not find out if there is one in your community?

Little Steven
for Artists United Against Apartheid
November 1, 1985

"Since 1652, when whites first entered South Africa, they have inflicted racial oppression on the blacks living there. The whites are composed of two main groups: The Afrikaners (those of Dutch ancestry) and the English (those of British ancestry). Because of superior weapons, the Europeans were able to win the continual wars they waged against the African population. The whites stripped the blacks of their land and livelihood. From the beginning all black resistance was brutally crushed, and blacks were forced to submit to laws established and controlled by the whites. By 1948, the National Party, dominated by the Afrikaners, was elected to power by the white minority on a platform of further strengthening white supremacy. Under this government, South Africa has institutionalized its oppressive policies to maintain total white control."

The Washington Office on Africa Educational Fund

This pedestrian, who refused to move fast enough out of Cape Town centre, was clubbed to the ground and ordered to get out by a baton-wagging policeman. *(Photo: UPI/Bettman Newsphotos)*

*"Sun City is an Afrikaner's paradise
in a black man's nightmare."*
—Eddie Amoo, musician, 1982

Sun City
The Glitter of Apartheid

Sun City is a $90-million Las Vegas-like pleasure resort stuck in the vast rural poverty of Bophuthatswana, one of the so-called "independent homelands" of South Africa. Featuring a casino, an artificial lake, soft-porn movies, discotheques, and scantily clad chorus girls, the enormous complex boasts a Superbowl—a large auditorium that regularly attracts big-name international entertainers and athletes, lured there by exorbitant fees and South Africa's assurances that the audience—indeed, the homeland of Bophuthatswana—is not a part of the apartheid system.

A tourist attraction which caters to the white South Africans who travel there, Sun City is exhibited as a showcase of the South African government. In reality, living conditions are harsh for the blacks who have been forcibly relocated to Bophuthatswana, and independence from apartheid and South Africa is merely an illusion. Because most blacks can't afford the high ticket prices at the Superbowl, often a few token tickets are given to them for free in order that the entertainers can perform before a "mixed" audience.

The United Nations and other anti-apartheid organizations have long advocated a cultural and sports boycott of South Africa and the resort. But Sun City continues to attract many international entertainers; perhaps, for some, it is the outrageous fees, perhaps, for others, it is ignorance of the realities of life for blacks in the homelands that contributes to their decision to perform there. Thus, Little

Steven and the fifty-three other musicians who form the Artists United Against Apartheid made the *Sun City* record so that entertainers as well as the public can learn the truth about South Africa's apartheid policies and phoney homelands. As Little Steven has said, "To forcibly relocate people is bad enough, but to erect a $90-million showplace to celebrate their imprisonment is beyond all conscience."

The Sun City complex plays a significant role in the South African effort to break out of its political isolation and win back foreign favor by camouflaging the reality of a system whose intent is not desegregation but the creation of an all-white South Africa. In 1978, Connie Mulder, the Minister of Bantu Administration and Development, said of the removal of blacks to homelands like Bophuthatswana, "If our policy is taken to its logical conclusion as far as the black people are concerned, there will not be one black man with South African citizenship. . . . Every black man in South Africa will eventually be accommodated in some independent new state in this honourable way and there will no longer be a moral obligation on this parliament to accommodate these people politically."

But the removal of blacks to barren, poverty-stricken homelands, stripping away all their rights to economic and political participation in South Africa, is an injustice that is an integral part of the disgrace of apartheid.

"The South African's government policy is to preserve white power through its legalized system of racism known as apartheid. The grand design of apartheid is the long term plan to forcibly remove blacks from their homes and place them in barren reserves called 'bantustans.' All blacks who are con-

sidered 'unnecessary' to the apartheid labor system are forced to live in these desolate and forgotten wastelands which make up only 13 percent of South Africa's land. Thus, although whites make up only 16 percent of the total population, they control 87 percent of the land. The white-controlled land includes all of the country's most fertile farms, cities and rich mineral deposits. The 13 percent of the land which makes up the bantustans is barren, soil eroded and not suitable for farming or cattle raising.

"The South African government forces blacks to live in these bantustans through a policy of forced removals. Between 1960 and 1984, the South African government [has] removed over 3½ million blacks from the 'white areas' to the bantustans. If communities resist a government-planned removal, even though they legally own the land on which they live, they are taken from their home—often at gunpoint—and their homes, churches and schools are bulldozed to the ground by the government. Entire families are taken to their designated bantustan and dumped there on small plots of land with only a tin toilet to mark their new 'address.'

"The white South African government's strategy is to divide the black people by their ethnic origin and force them into ten separate bantustans. Blacks cannot leave these bantustans without permission from the white government. The white government has declared four of these bantustans 'independent' . . .and stripped the black citizens [there] of their South African citizenship. No country in the world has recognized these bantustans as legitimate governments. Their so-called 'leaders' are hand-picked and paid by the South African government, which controls their defense, economic policy and monetary system. The bantustan 'officials' have only an advisory role, no real power or control. They are simply a front to hide the true character of the bantustans as concentration camps.

"Apartheid has created a labor system in which Africans must 'migrate' from the bantustans to work and live in the 'white areas' away from their families. The system is designed to create a pool of cheap labor and to ensure a steady flow of black labor from the rural areas to the urban areas. The government ensures that there are no jobs in the bantustans or any viable means for blacks to support themselves. Therefore, blacks are forced to accept any job offered them no matter what the working conditions or salary level.

"For blacks who find jobs in the 'white areas,' living conditions are oppressive. Workers are forced to live in single-sex hostels away from their families. They can only return to their families once or twice a year. These hostels are cramped and disease-ridden and destroy workers' dignity. Workers must support themselves and their far-off families on their meager salaries. If they lose their jobs they are dumped back in the bantustans. This policy ensures a poorly paid, steady supply of black labor for white South Africa.

"Another tragedy of forced removals is that it not only means the loss of jobs or the prospects of getting one, but it also destroys black families. Even if the entire family is resettled onto a bantustan, the conditions there are so squalid that the men must return to the 'white areas' to find work to prevent their families from starving. The daily economic reality for the vast majority of people left living in the bantustans (mainly women and children) is the struggle to survive on the meager corn and millet produced on poor and eroded land. Half of the children in the bantustans die before they reach the age of five. These areas contain no adequate housing, education or health facilities.

"Many women and children, in an effort to escape these conditions, ignore the stringent 'pass laws' prohibiting them from joining their husbands

and fathers in the 'white areas' and settle in large squatter camps on the edges of urban centers. The government's response has been swift and brutal. Squatter camps have been teargassed, bulldozed to the ground with the inhabitants beaten, arrested, fined, and dumped back in the desolate bantustans. But men and women continue to take this risk to find jobs or be near their loved ones.

"The bantustan policy of the South African government is a political version of the 'divide and rule' strategy. The purpose of this policy is to divide the black population into ethnic groups and separate them from each other to prevent them from mounting political opposition to apartheid. The government intends to move all the blacks out of 'white South Africa' to the bantustans by the year 2000, in order to make South Africa a totally white country where blacks can claim no political rights at all. The bantustan policy also serves to break institutional ties which hold the black population together—family, schools and the church. This makes it difficult for the blacks to launch a united struggle against apartheid."

(The Washington Office on Africa Educational Fund)

"Bophuthatswana [one of the ten bantustans] . . . has become internationally known as the home of the casino resort complex, Sun City. . . .Diversions forbidden elsewhere in South Africa flourish at Sun City. Yet behind this luxurious facade, the people of Bophuthatswana live in terrible poverty and the bantustan itself plays a central role in South Africa's apartheid system. . . .

"Bophuthatswana is the showcase bantustan, and proudly boasts a bill of rights. On paper it guarantees equality before the law, the right to freedom from torture and inhuman and degrading punishment and the right to freedom and liberty. But in reality, opposition is curtailed. The government maintains

the power of detention without trial and the right to declare any organization illegal. . . .The puppet leaders of the bantustans play their part, insisting that they are doing away with apartheid. The African majority knows better, understands that the bantustans are themselves apartheid. They will not be satisfied until they have equal access to the wealth of South Africa and full political rights in a unitary state."

(Richard Knight, September 1984, Southern Africa Perspectives, *"Black Dispossession in South Africa: The Myth of Bantustan Independence")*

In response to worldwide pressure, the South African government has announced its intention to relax certain restrictions imposed by apartheid, perhaps even to provide dual citizenship to the Africans living in the "independent" homelands. But black leaders have consistently denounced these "reforms," saying, "they polish our chains but won't remove them." Citizenship without power is meaningless. The South African government refuses to make specific promises regarding reform; instead it succumbs to pressure through propaganda and the construction of elaborate plans which mask South Africa's intent to retain absolute control in the hands of the white minority.

The Artists United Against Apartheid have contributed to the *Sun City* album their own special plea to the conscience of performers tempted by Sun City's facade and alluringly exorbitant fees. "Our song targets Sun City," explains Little Steven, who has visited South Africa, "but we use Sun City as a symbol of the whole apartheid system, with its program of forcibly relocating Africans into barren, artificial homelands, stripping them of their rights and economic sustenance. . . .Just as many of us sung out on behalf of the victims of Africa's famine, so we are singing out also for those hungry for freedom."

"SUN CITY"
words and music by Little Steven
© 1985 Solidarity Music

We're rockers and rappers united and strong (Run-DMC)
We're here to talk about South Africa, we don't like what's going on (Melle Mel & Duke Bootee)
It's time for some justice, it's time for the truth (Afrika Bambaataa & Kurtis Blow)
We've realized there's only one thing we can do (Big Youth & all rappers)

I ain't gonna play Sun City

Relocation to phoney homelands (David Ruffin)
Separation of families I can't understand (Pat Benatar)
23 million can't vote because they're black (Eddie Kendrick)
We're stabbing our brothers and sisters in the back (Bruce Springsteen)

I ain't gonna play Sun City

Our government tells us we're doing all we can (George Clinton)
Constructive engagement is Ronald Reagan's plan (Joey Ramone)
Meanwhile people are dying and giving up hope (Jimmy Cliff & Daryl Hall)
This quiet diplomacy ain't nothing but a joke (Darlene Love)

I ain't gonna play Sun City

It's time to accept our responsibility (Bonnie Raitt)
Freedom is a privilege, nobody rides for free (Ruben Blades & John Oates)
Look around the world baby it can't be denied (Lou Reed)
Why are we always on the wrong side (Bobby Womack)

I ain't gonna play Sun City

Bophuthatswana is far away (Run-DMC)
But we know it's in South Africa no matter what they say (Kurtis Blow & Africa Bambaataa)
You can't buy me, I don't care what you pay (Duke Bootee, Melle Mel & Afrika Bambaataa)
Don't ask me Sun City because I ain't gonna play (Linton Kwesi Johnson & all rappers)

I ain't gonna play Sun City

Relocation to phoney homelands (Jackson Browne & Bob Dylan)
Separation of families I can't understand (Peter Garrett)
23 million can't vote because they're black (Nona Hendryx & Kashif)
We're stabbing our brothers and sisters in the back (Bono)

"I was told (by the policemen) to give them whatever information I had on the political movement in South Africa. I refused, telling them that I had no information whatsoever to give them. A bag was pulled over my head and tied at my knees. I was then lifted by my feet and swung in the air like a pendulum, with my head knocking the ground every time, with every swing. . . .the policemen lit a match and threatened to burn me if I refused to give information. . . .I was told they were going to pass electric shocks through my body. . . .This they did for intervals of from three to five minutes. That went on for an hour and a half. . .I was. . .pushed through a window with my body hanging outside and they held me by my two feet. Every now and again they would release one foot. We were on the third floor of the building. After some time they pulled me back into the room. They again asked me to give them the information they wanted and when I refused again they beat me up and threw me on the floor, kicking me and using their fists every so often. . ."

United Nations pamphlet, A Crime Against Humanity

Under the state of emergency which was declared in July 1985, magistrates and police officers were granted authority to use or authorize force, including force resulting in death, if people refused to heed instructions given in a loud voice. *(Photo: Reuters/Bettman Newsphotos)*

SUN CITY THE MAKING OF THE RECORD

For almost forty years, world leaders and dignitaries have graced receptions in the Dag Hammarskjold Library in the penthouse of one of the United Nations buildings—but rarely has the U.N. played host to a group anything like the one that showed up on October 30, 1985.

That afternoon, the library was filled with the likes of Little Steven Van Zandt, Run-DMC, Joey Ramone, Ruben Blades, Afrika Bambaataa, Darlene Love, Stiv Bator, and Duke Bootee—a jagged cross-section of rockers, rappers, punkers, and *salseros* from the streets of urban New York. These musicians were present not because they were exceptionally famous (some are, some aren't) but because they were among the participants in the creation of a most extraordinary record: *Sun City*, by Artists United Against Apartheid.

Most often, celebrities and musicians come to the United Nations in order to be honored for acts of charity, but Artists United Against Apartheid was different. These performers had come not to receive but to give: Van Zandt and the project's other organizers—Arthur Baker, Rick Dutka, Owen Epstein, and Danny Schechter—presented the first pressing of their record, *Sun City,* to the Secretary-General of the United Nations and to the chairman of the Special Committee Against Apartheid.

The United Nations reception vividly and directly symbolized the commitment of 54 musicians from six continents to help end the ghastly system of racism and injustice that the South African government calls apartheid. That the presentation ceremony was taking place in the United States, whose government provides the indispensable political, strategic, and economic support without which apartheid could not stand, was a piece of irony that the musicians fully appreciated. In the U.S., the brutal truths about South Africa's apartheid system and its forced relocation ("homelands") project, both of which are symbolized by Sun City—a resort complex located in one of the homelands—are rarely explained in the media. So, in the end, "Sun City" was more than just a consciousness-raising project about apartheid and an act of determination by popular musicians. It also called attention to racism around the globe, and perhaps especially in the United States, the homeland of the majority of the "Sun City" performers.

When the record presentation ceremony was over, TV screens around the room lit up for the first-ever showing of the *Sun City* video clip. The array of singers and musicians who appeared on those screens was awesome; Artists United Against Apartheid is probably the most diverse group of musicians ever assembled for any purpose.

Playing a trumpet obbligato over the opening bars was jazz legend Miles Davis, setting an angry, painful mood. He was followed by a host of greats: reggae giants Jimmy Cliff and Big Youth; salsa kings Ray Barretto and Ruben Blades; hordes of rappers led by Grandmaster Melle Mel, Duke Bootee, Afrika Bambaataa, Kurtis Blow, and Run-DMC; rock superstars Bruce Springsteen, Bob Dylan, Ringo Starr, Pat Benatar, and Pete Townshend; George Clinton, the master of funk; and such ordinarily elusive figures as Peter Gabriel, Tony Williams, and Lou Reed. From Australia came Peter Garrett of Midnight Oil; from Africa itself, Sonny Okosuns of Nigeria, as well as Malopoets and Via Afrika, South African groups who had paid the heavy price of exile for the very convictions that caused *Sun City* to be made.

It wasn't simply the big-name talent that made

the *Sun City* video a stunning experience. The visual presentation itself left viewers reeling. The video led off with scenes and narration from a mock South African promotional film that made it clear just what a fraud Sun City, the internationally oriented casino, resort, and arena complex, really is. Sun City pays hundreds of thousands—sometimes millions—to pop stars who agree to appear there in defiance of the U.N.-sponsored boycott of all cultural and sports appearances in South Africa. Performers appear at Sun City on the dubious grounds that Sun City is not located in South Africa but in the black "homeland" of Bophuthatswana. Like the other "homelands," to which millions of South African blacks have been forcibly relocated, the isolated areas that make up Bophuthatswana are completely surrounded by South Africa, and its "independent" status is recognized by no other nation on earth.

In the video, the first scenes of Sun City's poolside sunshine and luxurious night life are immediately undercut. At first, the edge was supplied by the narration, delivered in an unwaveringly prim South African accent, spieling the facts about the conditions of black life in South Africa—the very facts that Sun City was created to conceal. But that edge was sharpened as the music began its shuddering awakening, hissing voices snapping "Ahhh Sun City!" as the drums crashed in. Suddenly, Run-DMC appeared on the screen, followed by Grandmaster Melle Mel, Duke Bootee, Afrika Bambaataa, and Kurtis Blow, all declaring:

> *We're rockers and rappers united and strong*
> *We're here to talk about South Africa, we*
> *   don't like what's going on*
> *It's time for some justice; it's time for the*
> *   truth*
> *We've realized there's only one thing we can*
> *   do*

L-r: Charlie Wilson, Little Steven, Nona Hendryx, and Herbie Hancock. *(Photo: David Seelig/Star File)*

Little Steven. *(Photo: David Seelig/Star File)*

L-r: Arthur Baker, Miles Davis and Bonnie Raitt. *(Photo: David Seelig/Star File)*

Ray Barretto. *(Photo: Chase Roe)*

Jam Master Jay from Run-DMC. *(Photo: David Seelig/Star File)*

Herbie Hancock. *(Photo: David Seelig/Star File)*

The camera panned right, and there was Little Steven with Scorpio, another rapper, declaring:

I...
I...
I...
Ain't gonna play Sun City!

The screen virtually burst at the seams as images ripped and tore at one another: South Africa's Prime Minister P.W. Botha pitted against African National Congress leader Nelson Mandela; rocker Bruce Springsteen cruising down a New York City street in solidarity with Temptations' Eddie Kendrick and David Ruffin; shots of Sun City resort life inter-cut with depictions of the squalor in which black South Africans live; ecstatic footage of the entire "Sun City" crew dancing and declaiming in New York City's Washington Square Park bouncing off film from South African riots; and shots of the battle in South Africa bumping up against footage of dem-onstrators being attacked by cops and guard dogs in Birmingham, Alabama.

At the end, when *Sun City* had built and spent its fury, the image crossfades once more to South Africa, to hundreds of demonstrators singing "Nkosi Sikeleli Africa" ("God Bless Africa"), their national anthem, which although banned in South Africa is always sung at funerals and demonstrations anyway. Finally the clip froze on a single face, a child of apartheid, living like a prisoner, his eyes expressing all of the sadness and unanswered ques-tions of oppression, a tangible symbol of what the seven minutes of video furor had been about.

Even for those already familiar with "the facts" about South African apartheid, *Sun City* and its re-markable video drove the story home more deeply, making the horror real and unforgettable. That sense of horror is the energy source behind the music, too, for no one who directly and honestly confronts the

THE SHARPEVILLE MASSACRE

On March 21, 1960, sixty-nine people were killed in what came to be known as the Sharpeville Massacre when South African police opened fire on men, women, and children who were peacefully protesting against the pass laws. A week later a State of Emergency was declared, and 22,000 people were detained or arrested. At the same time, the Unlawful Organizations Act was passed on the same day that the African National Congress and the Pan-Africanist Congress called for a boycott of work in order to observe a day of mourning. Under this act, both organizations were declared illegal and forced underground.

March 21, 1960. The aftermath of the Sharpeville Massacre. *(Photo: UPI/Bettman Newsphotos)*

perversion of humanity that is the essence of apartheid can possibly tolerate its existence.

The story of "Sun City" really begins with Little Steven Van Zandt, an Italian-American whose Dutch surname is not far removed from those of the Afrikaners who colonized South Africa in the seventeenth century and of their descendents, who, beginning in 1948, imposed the specific conditions now called apartheid. Van Zandt, thirty-five, has been a professional musician all his adult life, working in a variety of bands in his native New Jersey, leading the E Street Band for his friend Bruce Springsteen, and producing such artists as Southside Johnny, Ronnie Spector, and Gary "U.S." Bonds before beginning his solo career in 1983.

Van Zandt's interest in South Africa was awakened one night in 1980 in a Hollywood revival theater, the kind of place where the music between shows is provided by the projectionist's custom-made cassettes. This projectionist had the good taste to play "Biko," a Peter Gabriel song about Steve Biko, the thirty-one-year-old black leader murdered in 1977 while in South African security police detention. (Biko was at that time the forty-sixth such person to die while in custody of the security police; the number of such deaths has grown steadily every year.)

"It moved me in an abstract, purely emotional way," Van Zandt remembers—and no wonder. "Biko" is a slow and mournful song as befits a funeral dirge. (It begins and ends with South Africans singing during funeral marches.) Its combination of relentless drumbeats and droning ominous guitar with bagpipes skirling in the background would be fascinating in any context. The words Gabriel sings add another layer of mystery; he doesn't really explain what has happened to Biko— he just states that "the man is dead." Only at the end

does the singer state his case:

*You can blow out a candle, but you can't
    blow out a fire
Once the flame begins to catch, the wind
    will blow it higher...
And the eyes of the world are watching now.*

"'Biko' really planted the seed," Van Zandt says. "After that, I always had that song on the tape before my live shows, it always stayed with me." Meantime, Van Zandt was having his eyes opened by touring outside the United States for the first time and coming face to face with his country's role in fostering and bolstering repressive regimes. Van Zandt resolved to do something that would awaken his own countrymen to what their government does in their name and to make clear to the rest of the world that not all Americans agreed with making "endless enemies" of every liberation movement in the world. One result was his second solo album, *Voice of America,* released in mid-1984, whose songs focused on precisely those topics.

Through EMI Records, the record label that released *Voice of America,* Van Zandt traveled to South Africa. "The record company down there [South Africa] did a very smart thing," he recalls. "They sent a white guy and a black guy to this convention in Los Angeles, and I happened to be at the same hotel. I thought, 'Now that is interesting!' I started talking to them, and I told them I wanted to write about South Africa." One of them, Peter Ritchie (he turned out to be English and has since moved back to England), had spent most of his life in South Africa and encouraged Steven to come down. Later, when Van Zandt arrived in Johannesburg, Ritchie was instrumental in setting up meetings and showing him around.

At the time, Van Zandt was himself somewhat skeptical of the need for a United Nations cultural

and sports boycott of South Africa, which had been formalized in 1980 but was both poorly publicized and rarely explained in the United States until four or five years later. "I had a lot of questions to ask about the boycott [before I went]," Van Zandt says. "Partly because I didn't realize what stage the war was at, that the war was already on and it was already late in the day. After all, there was nothing in the papers here in the States. I thought maybe there was a more effective plan, a more selective boycott, all kinds of ideas that would advance a peaceful solution. It wasn't until I got there that I understood that I wasn't incorrect in my thinking so much as too late.

"I wanted to play there very much. I thought that with my songs, what more appropriate place to play them could there be? But once I got there and talked to the black community, it was obviously too late." He pauses and laughs. "So I told 'em I'd be back Independence Day."

In fact, Van Zandt returned to South Africa sooner than he had originally planned. Some of the meetings he had wanted to arrange on his first trip were harder to put together than he had imagined. "Especially since I had three strikes against me already: I was white, I was American, and I had a Dutch name—it didn't do any good to try to explain that I was an Italian-American who had been adopted by my father. Plus, I was a rock musician, an entertainer to them, which didn't help either."

Nevertheless, with the help of the friends he had made in South Africa, Van Zandt persevered, and on his second journey, in the autumn of 1984, he was able to speak with representatives of UDF (the United Democratic Front), AZAPO (Azanian People's Organization), two directors of the South African Council of Churches, and Beyers Naude, the seventy-year-old Dutch Reformed Church minister who is probably the leading Afrikaner opponent of

Little Steven and Darlene Love. *(Photo: David Seelig/Star File)*

Tina B. *(Photo: David Seelig/Star File)*

Malopoets and Little Steven *(Photo: David Seelig/Star File)*

David Ruffin. *(Photo: Reuven Kopitchinski)*

Jimmy Cliff. *(Photo: David Seelig/Star File)*

Scorpio and Arthur Baker. *(Photo: Bill Adler)*

Daryl Hall. *(Photo: David Seelig/Star File)*

apartheid and who later assumed leadership of the SACC when Bishop Desmond Tutu was prevented from doing so by the government. He also met with the head of the South African Sports Institute and with leaders of Black Sash, the free legal aid organization, as well as with numerous doctors, lawyers, teachers, and trade unionists.

"It was very hard to adapt to the culture as you must to get any objective work done. There's a certain attitude on a daily basis that you're constantly confronted with—that thing between blacks and whites, even with white people who hate apartheid or are extremely liberal," Steven says. "You have to constantly discipline yourself to *not* react, because if you heard somebody talking that way here, you'd absolutely react—you'd probably punch them in the mouth. It's just constant condescension and arrogance. Sometimes they don't even realize it.

"And it causes so much tension—you can't ever relax, you constantly feel like the sky is about to fall, you're the only one who knows, and no one will believe you. You go ten miles down the road and there's Soweto; the riots had already started so people were being killed every day, and yet in the white neighborhoods nothing was going on, no one was concerned. Just picture a regular, white, suburban neighborhood. You start to feel like you're insane."

For Little Steven, the ultimate shock came during his junket to Sun City itself. Although ostensibly in a different nation (the homeland of Bophuthatswana), Sun City is conveniently located only a few hours' drive from Johannesburg. The main strip leading to the resort is slightly upgraded, but Sun City itself is surrounded by a ghetto which gives the lie to the notion that the theoretically "black ruled" homelands are an improvement over black life in the rest of South Africa. As Van Zandt says, Bophuthatswana is "more or less representative of the homelands: it's way out in the middle of nowhere, very

desolate, there's no work, no schools, no agriculture, no hospitals, nothing."

Van Zandt found that visiting Sun City was the absolute limit his system could take. "We went and the group Queen was playing there. You walk around, and you're transported to yet another world. It's very much like Las Vegas or Atlantic City, except there's just one big hotel and casino and there's an arena attached to it. A mile away is the shanty town where people actually live.

"The mind-boggling aspects of it really got me there. I got sick, as sick as I've ever gotten in my life. The doctor said it was not something I ate or drank, it was just psychological—the old tourist-in-hell syndrome."

Depressing as the experience had been, Little Steven did manage to write most of an album while in South Africa, much of it based on his experiences and observations of the misery of apartheid. He returned home to a certain amount of business turmoil, however, and having left EMI and broken up his band, wasn't really certain how to get the right record made.

Sometime around March 1985, Steven ran into Danny Schechter, a journalist and television producer who made his early reputation as "The News Dissector" at Boston's WBCN, where he was one of the most innovative broadcasters ever to wield a splicing blade. Schechter originally met up with Van Zandt in order to interview him, and their common interests soon made them friends. "Danny really inspired the thing," Steven says. "He said, 'It's a shame you haven't started the album yet. It would be great to get something out this year.' Finally, he said, 'Why don't you just do a single?'"

Schechter says that he was especially concerned because the only images of Africa in the U.S. media at that time were those of the famine in Ethiopia.

Little was being said about the drive for freedom at the other end of the continent. It was during these months, of course, that Bob Geldof and others began organizing the massive famine relief efforts that resulted in Band Aid, Live Aid, and USA for Africa. Van Zandt and Schechter hoped to give a different sense of African reality and to pull together something that fused charitable concerns with those for human rights. They were looking for a team of international musicians that would include "artists from all cultures, areas, and races."

Van Zandt and Schechter strategized during occasional conversations throughout the spring. Eventually, they determined several principles on which such a record should be made: It should show solidarity with the Black South African freedom movement, and it should focus on the cultural boycott, because it was important to feature artists talking to artists as well as to generally educate the public about the issue.

The two spent a long time considering one particular aspect of the lyrics: Since there were many well-known artists who had deliberately and sometimes repeatedly violated the boycott, yet got away scot-free when they came back home, Schechter felt that it would be appropriate to name names. Little Steven wasn't so sure.

As a news producer, Schechter told Van Zandt that the political statement would have to be his. He would be able to help out only with the charitable aspects of the project and could not cover it in any way—lest there be even the appearance of a conflict of interest. It was Little Steven who figured out the actual shape of the song and its political thrust.

In the meantime, Steven was doing some songwriting with producer Arthur Baker, including "You Don't Have to Cry" for reggae star Jimmy Cliff and "Addiction" for Baker's own solo album. (Both songs had political lyrics.)

Baker, now in his early thirties, grew up in Boston and came to New York in the early 1980s. There he discovered a genius for mixing and remixing contemporary dance records, using the modern recording studio console as a type of musical instrument. His work with Afrika Bambaataa, New Order, Cyndi Lauper, Bruce Springsteen, and Freez helped redefine dance music in the 80s. Like Van Zandt, Baker was a white kid with an intense interest in black music and a previously hidden itch to do something about racism.

Baker has his own Manhattan studio, Shakedown Sound, and he'd already offered Van Zandt free use of it during off hours to work up his new material. That music was in the works when Van Zandt decided to travel to Nicaragua with his friend Jackson Browne. When Steven got back in touch, Baker was finishing up an album with the pop group Face to Face. That album's sessions were wrapped up in political questions as well. Steven joined in the discussion; Steven argued that new bands should be able to write what they want instead of being molded by record company executives. He urged the band to include "America's Dream" on their album, a song the company said was too political. Arthur felt a balance was needed. Steven said, balance yes, compromise never.

They didn't return to the topic of Africa until mid-June, when Steven called while Arthur was working with Cyndi Lauper on a remix of "Goonies Are Good Enough." Oddly, at the time Lauper and Baker were already discussing African music, because she was convinced that "Goonies" was somehow African sounding. Van Zandt came by later that same night bearing a demo that had been recorded the previous evening at the Upper West Side apartment of his keyboardist/assistant Zöe Yanakis and his equipment handler Ben Newberry. This original, skeletal version of the song featured

Bono and Bruce Springsteen. *(Photo: David Seelig/Star File)*

L-r: Peter Wolf, Joey Ramone, Darlene Love, and Jimmy Cliff. *(Photo: Reuven Kopitchinski)*

"The Bantu must be guided to serve his own community in all respects. There is no place for him in the European community above the level of certain forms of labour. Within his own community, however, all doors are open...Until now he has been subjected to a school system which drew him away from his own community and misled him by showing him the green pastures of European society in which he was not allowed to graze."

Dr. H.F. Verwoerd, Minister of Native Affairs (later Prime Minister),
7 June 1954

For black South Africans, education means crowded classrooms (during 1982–83, the ratio of black students to teachers was 42.7 to 1, compared to 18.2 to 1 for whites) and sometimes not enough classroom space. Black South African teachers are paid lower salaries by the government, which spent R1,385 (1,385 Rands, the African monetary unit) per white student and only R115.9 (115.9 Rands) per African student during 1982–83. The result is an illiteracy rate of 40 to 50 percent among Africans, thus effectively keeping the African population at the bottom of society.

The Apartheid Handbook, *Roger Omond, Penguin Books*

In Bophuthatswana, an empty room with a crude chalkboard constitutes a classroom. In many areas throughout South Africa there are simply no schools at all. *(Photo: The Africa Fund)*

Apartheid Education

"Education under apartheid is both racially segregated and racist in orientation. It is designed to give blacks an inferior education to keep them powerless. Education for whites is both free and compulsory. Blacks must pay for their education [the cost of books and fees] and it is not required."

"The blacks in South Africa have tried repeatedly to obtain quality education. In 1976, students in the black township of Soweto boycotted schools and held protests because the government wanted to educate them only in Afrikaans, the language of white Afrikaners, excluding English. To know only Afrikaans would lead to a further elimination of employment opportunities for blacks. However, the police responded to the students' peaceful protests with violence, shooting, and killing 600 unarmed black schoolchildren over the weeks of protest."

The Washington Office on Africa Educational Fund

The town of Soweto continues to be the center of rebellion. Trucks return a few of the 800 students who were released after their arrest during the August 1985 police raids on Soweto schools *(Photo: Reuters/Bettman Newsphotos)*

Van Zandt, Newberry, and Yanakis, plus a drum machine. Baker liked the song so much that he expressed an interest in getting involved. The pair immediately decided to record a more elaborate demo the next evening, June 15, at Shakedown.

"Ninety percent of what we recorded that first night is on the finished record," Baker says. "All the drums, including the DX7 log drum [which is just a preset], Steve's guitars, Richard Scher's clavinet, and the other keyboards. In one or two sessions, all the music was done. Then we wanted someone to duet with Steve, and Will Downing was around, so we asked him to come in. The original background vocals were done by BLT"—a group Arthur Baker frequently works with, which consists of B.J. Nelson, Lotte Golden, and Tina B, who doubles as Baker's wife.

The demo complete, Arthur and Steven sat up for the rest of the night and put together a "wish list" of fifty or sixty—by Baker's estimate—artists that they hoped would become involved in the project. (Baker says that about eighty percent of those artists eventually did come aboard.) Over the next few weeks, as they refined their concept of what "Sun City" should be, that list was remade over and over again.

"It was obviously just a fantasy," says Little Steven modestly. "We had no record label or anything. We didn't know who the hell was gonna respond." But beneath the fantasy were several substantial goals, ones that somewhat belied Steven's early admonition to Baker: "Let's try and have some fun."

"Originally, we thought we'd try to put together a record with an alternative group of musicians—less mainstream, more of a street record," says Baker. "It was already a street *sound*. Nobody ever said it this way, but we thought we might get some people who had things to say but who would never

Gil Scott-Heron and Little Steven. *(Photo: David Seelig/Star File)*

Sonny Okosuns. *(Photo: David Seelig/Star File)*

Little Steven. *(Photo: David Seelig/Star File)*

Tina B and Peter Wolf. *(Photo: Steve Goldstein)*

Little Steven and Big Youth. *(Photo: David Seelig/Star File)*

George Clinton. *(Photo: David Seelig/Star File)*

have been asked to be on Live Aid or USA for Africa—people who express their social concerns all the time."

That group certainly included the rappers, especially Run-DMC, who had supported student strikers that spring at Columbia and Cornell universities by performing for them during campus demonstrations over South African disinvestment. Van Zandt adds that the mixture of styles and personalities that was eventually achieved "had to do with my and Arthur's taste. We gave no consideration whatsoever as to how successful somebody was, just how soulful. Every artist was equally important to us—it's just that some of them sell lots of records and some of them don't."

There was a second incentive for going that route: They needed to work with people who were readily available. Neither Van Zandt nor the "Sun City" project had a record label, which meant that every dollar that was spent had to come out of pockets that weren't exceptionally deep. Without corporate support, it was impossible to fly artists into New York from all over the world, as some of the charity events had done. On the other hand, that didn't mean that they had to think small. Both Baker and Van Zandt regularly spoke to and worked with superstars, and many musicians were based in New York. "From the day we put the first track down, Steve and I both said, 'Wouldn't it be wild to get Miles Davis to play trumpet over this log drum?' "

The demo justified all their hopes. It is a bone-crushing piece of music, and stripped to the basics is more spare and driving than the finished project—it's a screaming, careening piece of modern urban funk that seems to have come in on a time loop from a land where Sly and the Family Stone and Grandmaster Melle Mel cavort with the Disciples of Soul at Stevie Wonder's house.

A few weeks later, Baker described it as the best

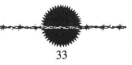

thing he'd ever done. Even after the *Sun City* album was released, Rick Dutka, Vice-President of Tommy Boy Records, who had joined the project after the demo was cut, was joking that the demo should have been included on the album. Downing's booming, Bobby Womack-like voice shivers the spine, and Van Zandt gives a soulful, untethered performance that is probably the most outstanding of his career. It's a performance he'd been pointing to since 1984's "Vote!" (his anti-Reagan election song which nobody would release in America), which served as a prototype for the thematic twelve-inch that *Sun City* started out to be.

In fact, the demo of "Sun City" presented only one problem, stemming from the idea that the song should name names of South African boycott violators. In the midst of the demo, the music falls away to just the log drum and BLT, who taunt:

> *Linda Ronstadt, how could you do that?*
> *Rod Stewart, tell me that you didn't do it*
> *Julio Iglesias, you oughta be ashamed to*
> *   show your face*
> *Queen and the O'Jays, what you got to say?*

The verse presented several problems, some practical, some political, some ethical. "I just decided I didn't want to make value judgments on people who went there," Van Zandt says. "People have gone for all kinds of reasons. The important thing is that they not go back."

In the first place, while the O'Jays *had* played Sun City, they had later made a statement of apology through the United Nations, which is all that is required to have one's name removed from the list of boycott violators. And the O'Jays' apology was elaborate and embarrassed, more authentic in tone than most. This only heightened the overriding problem with the verse: that it singled out only a few boycott violators, while a dozen others who had played Sun City or otherwise violated the boycott were not named. (Elton John, Ray Charles, and Frank Sinatra, for instance, were not named.)

Additionally, the verse tended to throw off the emphasis of the song, changing it from a positive statement of commitment to ending apartheid to a lambasting of boycott violators (not that they didn't deserve a lambasting). By consensus, everyone finally agreed that the song should *not* name names.

By the time that consensus was reached, however, about eighty cassettes of the demo, which included the offending lyrics, had been rough-mixed by engineer Jeff Hendrickson and sent out by Yanakis. This engendered some mild controversy within the music community, but more important it made the newspapers, through Nelson George's "The Rhythm and the Blues" column in *Billboard*. From there, the story was picked up and syndicated; predictably, the reports focused almost solely on the idea of the song as an attack on boycott violators, without bothering to explain why the boycott was important or the basically positive message of the song—or, for that matter, the fact that the lyrics in question had already been dropped.

On the other hand, that was the only negative note. With very few exceptions, almost everybody who was sent a demo was willing—and even eager —to perform. "Me and Danny said, 'Maybe we'll get one person from each kind of music.' We definitely wanted to get rappers and rockers together," Van Zandt remembers. "But then we just started calling all the people we could think of. The response was so much more enthusiastic than I had expected. I mean, now it's fifty-four artists later, and we could still be recording."

The first to jump in were the rappers Run-DMC followed closely by Ruben Blades, Ray Barretto (the veteran conga player was in fact the first nonrapper to sign up), Peter Wolf, and

34

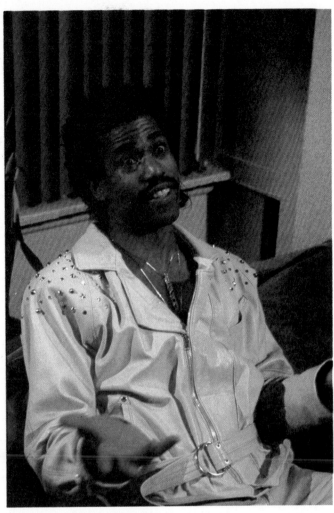

Kurtis Blow. *(Photo: Chase Roe)*

Scorpio. *(Photo: David Seelig/Star File)*

"Sun City's become a symbol of a society which is very oppressive and denies basic rights to the majority of its citizens. In a sense, Sun City is also a symbol of that society's right to entertain itself in any way that it wants to, and to basically try to buy us off, and to buy off world opinion."

—Jackson Browne

"I've always followed what was going on in South Africa—injustice, apartheid. So when they called me to put my voice on [*Sun City*], it wasn't something I even had to think about. It was like I had a chance to *do* something."

—Scorpio

Jamaican heroes Big Youth, Jimmy Cliff, Joey Ramone, Lou Reed, and Darlene Love.

Nevertheless, it took six weeks to pin things down firmly enough to begin the sessions. They finally got started on July 31, with a group that included Afrika Bambaataa, Melle Mel, and Duke Bootee. This session marked the beginning of one of the most complex recordings anyone has ever made. In the end, for this single song, 13 master tapes—a total of more than 300 separate tracks—were created.

Until very late in the process, each musician sang not just a single line ("We-Are-the-World" style), but rather three or four lines, or sometimes even the whole song, which vastly increased the amount of tracks that had to be sorted through before the final editing and mixing began. After some time Baker and Van Zandt were fairly certain whose lines went where, but even then, when an unusually special voice became available—Bobby Womack's, for example—they'd do another complete take of the song.

"We were originally looking for eight or ten other artists," Little Steven says. "I honestly didn't expect that many people to be committed to the issue. It was very exciting, because like most musicians, I spend most of my time doing things alone. You feel part of a musical community, but you really don't know, especially about an issue like this. You just don't. And to see that many people committed was wild."

As it turns out, he says, "We could have stopped recording after the first week because it was great already." By that time they'd added Blades, Cliff, Lou Reed, Joey Ramone, and Darlene Love. In addition, Jackson Browne had been contacted and a duplicate master was sent to his Los Angeles recording studio, Outpost. There, Browne, Darryl Hannah, Kevin McCormick, and Peter Garrett of Australia's

Midnight Oil laid down tracks and then sent the master along to Pat Benatar, who added her contribution at Cherokee Studios, where she was recording an album. Later, the tape would be sent back to LA for Bob Dylan, who had previously expressed his interest but had been busy with the FarmAid rehearsals and concert. The tape was returned—with Dylan's distinctive voice—to New York on the weekend of the final mix.

Enthusiasm among the musical community ran so high that new performers were constantly simply turning up. During Herbie Hancock's session, Little Steven got a call from keyboardist Richard Scher. Via Afrika, a group composed of three white South African women (whom Steven had previously met in South Africa), had flown in from South Africa the night before, having finally realized that there was no place for their assertive stance in an apartheid state. Without much planning (they had less than $100 among them), Via Afrika had simply decided to emigrate. They phoned Scher, whom they'd worked with previously, and he called Steven. Less than forty-eight hours after they'd gone into exile, Via Afrika were in the studio, making a record about the very forces that had driven them from their homeland.

Meanwhile, Van Zandt flew to London, where he caught up with Nona Hendryx and the outspoken Jamaican dub poet, Linton Kwesi Johnson. Stiv Bator of the Lords of the New Church (the postpunk band for whom Van Zandt had just produced two songs) and Michael Monroe of Hanoi Rocks also joined in, further diversifying the sound. Little Steven had also hoped to record Pete Townshend and Ringo Starr while he was in England, but though both had expressed an interest in performing "Sun City" they were both out of town that week. So it was back to London a week later to record Townshend at his Eel Pie Studios near his home in Twickenham, and Ringo at his Startling Sounds in the

L-r: Bruce Springsteen, David Ruffin, and Eddie Kendrick. *(Photo: Reuven Kopitchinski)*

Standing, l-r: John Davenport, Keith Le Blanc, and Arthur Baker; sitting, l-r: Little Steven, Chris Lord-Alge, and Tom Lord-Alge. *(Photo: David Seelig/Star File)*

Africans are forbidden to vote, buy or sell land in most areas, or choose where to live and work. Through the 317 laws that enforce the subjugation of Africans, they are legally deprived of any control over their lives. These laws, for example, permit the jailing of the government's opponents and allow the police to operate with impunity.

"The white government controls every black person through a sophisticated computer network requiring all blacks over the age of 16 to carry a 'passbook' at all times. The passbook contains fingerprints, a photograph, and employment records. If it is not produced upon demand, blacks are jailed and fined. More than 13 million Africans have been convicted of pass law offenses since the National Party came to power in 1948—almost 1,000 every day."

The Washington Office on Africa Educational Fund

(Opposite) The passbook which all blacks over the age of 16 must carry at all times, belongs to a man who is classified under Section H of the passbook as Zulu. The space for citizenship is left blank since the South African government considers him a citizen of KwaZulu, one of the homelands, even though he was born in South Africa. *(Photo reprinted with special permission from* Harper's Magazine © 1985)

REFERENCE BOOK.—BEWYSBOEK.

27 -06- 1977

WARNING: It is an offence for any person other than the one authorised or required by law to make any entry in this book.

WAARSKUWING: Dit is 'n oortreding vir enige persoon wat nie by wet daartoe gemagtig of verplig is nie, om enige inskrywing in hierdie boek aan te bring.

INDEX.—INDEKS.

A. (1) Residential address.
Woonadres.

(2) Administration.
Administrasie.

B. Employment.
Indiensneming.

C. General and hospital tax.
Algemene en hospitaalbelasting.

D. Local tax, levies and rates.
Plaaslike belasting en heffings.

E. Additional particulars under regulation 17 (1) (V), Chapter II, Bantu Labour Regulations, 1965.
Bykomende besonderhede volgens regulasie 17 (1) (V), Hoofstuk II, Bantoe-arbeidregulasies, 1965.

F. Driver's licences.
Bestuurderslisensies.

G. Licences to possess arms.
Lisensies om wapens te besit.

H. Personal particulars.
Persoonlike besonderhede.

KLERK VAN DIE BANTOESAKEKOMMIS-SARISHOF
E V A T O N
21 -06- 1977
PK. P.O. RESIDENSIA

1

Ascot countryside. Both men were already committed to anti-apartheid issues. Ringo told Steven that the Beatles had been asked to play South Africa twenty years ago but even then they were aware of apartheid. He'd been following the situation ever since. Townshend had for some time been a supporter of the Lincoln Trust, an anti-apartheid educational organization. Townshend introduced Steven to the director of The Lincoln Trust, ex-newspaper editor Donald Woods, the exiled South African author of *Biko,* a book about the slain African leader who had been Woods' close friend.

Ringo was recorded drumming with his twenty-two-year-old son, Zak Starkey, marking the first time that the former Beatle had ever performed with his son. The session was almost canceled because Zak's wife was in labor, about to deliver any minute. Fortunately, the baby waited out the session. Ringo, the first Beatle to achieve grandfatherhood, took the first pictures of the historic infant, which were beamed around the world and featured all three generations of the Starkey clan wearing Artists United Against Apartheid T-shirts.

Steven had also been trying to contact Bob Geldof. "We actually spoke through messages," he said. "He left a message at the hotel where I was staying, then I left a message where he was, and he just ended up at Eel Pie. Which was great of him because he was a very busy man then."

Geldof was not the only contributor to "Sun City" who was interested but difficult to track down. Bruce Springsteen, Van Zandt's oldest friend, was on the road all summer, and it seemed—at least from the outside—unlikely that he would be able to perform. Steven had talked to him earlier but hadn't said anything about it. On August 29, his show at Giants Stadium in New Jersey was canceled due to bad weather and Bruce came down that night and quietly put his part on.

Gil Scott-Heron—the singer who had spotlighted South Africa with the hit "Johannesburg" in 1975—was even more elusive. "From the moment we first started to record, I'd been searching for Gil. He's a very difficult man to find —I mean, we were calling phone booths and stuff. Finally, we tracked him down at a hotel in Martha's Vineyard. But the rooms didn't have any phones. So I called the desk and tried to explain what I wanted. At that moment, Gil's bass player was walking by, and he recognized my name from *No Nukes* [the anti-nuclear rally Van Zandt had performed with Springsteen in 1979]. So he took the call, and we got Gil. I mean, if he hadn't been buying a candy bar at that very instant, forget it!"

Scott-Heron had already planned to come to New York that Saturday night, to play aboard a Hudson River cruise boat, and by early Sunday afternoon, he turned up at the Hit Factory. Inside the studio, Scott-Heron quickly developed his "Let Me See Your I.D." rap while his group chimed in on the choruses. Rick Dutka was in the studio that night with his wife and four-month-old baby, Annie. When the baby started to cry, Dutka cringed. But Little Steven turned and said, "Zöe, get a mike on that kid. She's expressing what this record is all about more eloquently than we ever could." Annie was taken to the studio where a microphone was suspended above her face. She stared in quiet fascination for a couple of minutes, then cut loose with several hearty wails; this "universal cry of suffering" can be heard on the twelve-inch version of "Let Me See Your I.D."

From day one everyone had dreamed of getting Miles Davis to participate, but nobody had really thought that the reclusive trumpeter, one of the crowning glories of jazz and a private citizen to the ultimate extreme, was actually a likely candidate to join such a public and collaborative project. "Every-

John Oates. *(Photo: Heil Winoker)*

Bruce Springsteen and Little Steven. *(Photo: David Seelig/Star File)*

Front, l-r: Joey Ramone, Michael Monroe, and Stiv Bator. *(Photo: Reuven Kopitchinski)*

"I think racism is a disease of the spirit, and it's time for artists to take a stand, to help make others aware of what's going on and what needs to be changed. Traditionally, music has been used for escape, and I think it's about time we started using music to confront as well."

—Ruben Blades

body told me it was impossible," Little Steven now says, with a wry smile. "I just kept saying he'll be here until he showed up. It turned out that Miles's sound man was my old sound man from one of my tours. But in the end, it was obviously something that Miles wanted to talk about."

Ultimately, the task of corralling Davis fell to Schechter, and when he finally got through, Miles's response was simple: "When do you want me there?" But Davis failed to return any of Schechter's follow-up phone calls. Therefore, no one was quite sure who would attend the session that mid-August afternoon. Kashif and Bonnie Raitt were there, the latter having canceled a sound check for a crucial gig at the Ritz in order to sing.

"We're all getting ready to record Bonnie, who's on a very tight schedule because of the Ritz gig, and in walks Miles Davis," Schechter remembers. "He'd just gotten up and left the first day of rehearsals for *his* tour." As Davis took his place in the studio, no one quite knew what to do about the presence of the crew that up until then filmed all of the sessions. Knowing the vaunted Davis reputation for skittish behavior in the face of supplementary media, no one really wanted to ask Miles's permission: His presence seemed already too great a gift to risk losing him over this. But Danny Schechter marched boldly into the studio. "Listen, Miles, you don't mind if we film you like we've been doing with these sessions, do you?" "Bring it on, bring it on," Miles replied. bring it on," Miles replied.

What they brought him, inside his headphones, was simply the log drum track, without even the guide vocal. The idea was just to let him wing it, which he did in two takes, the first played with a mute, the second with the horn open. During both, he chewed gum.

"At the end of the first take, he started to mutter, 'You can't go in there, you're the wrong color,'"

Baker says. "We thought he was talking about the cameraman, and everybody freaked. But then we realized he was talking about South Africa. I said, 'Keep those tapes rolling.' When he was done, we all just looked at each other, and then Danny—you know Danny—walks out and says, 'That was really great. Could you do that rap again so we're sure we have it? We wanted to kill Danny." But Miles just smiled and went on re-doing his track.

From the beginning, Van Zandt and Baker had been encouraging the artists to expand upon their contribution to *Sun City*. "What was amazing to me was that the song wasn't gonna sound like the demo. Each artist brought something a little different," Schechter says. Even at the first session, the project was quickly becoming a spontaneous effort. "Melle Mel went out of the studio for fifteen minutes and came back with the perfect rap," Baker said. Then Mel laid it down in only two takes—the first was the keeper and became part of "Let Me See Your I.D."

Davis's version paved the way for what Arthur Baker half-jokingly referred to as "the jazz version," known on the *Sun City* LP as "The Struggle Continues." Davis became the bedrock, and at that time the producers fully expected the rest of the track to be supplied by keyboardist Herbie Hancock, who, after proving almost as hard to find as his mentor, came in a few days later. (Hancock had been working in Europe and only came back to the States to appear on the MTV Music Awards program. This would have proved far too late if the project had kept very close to what was somewhat laughably called its "schedule.")

Hancock was the first artist to play over the full track, and, according to Baker, he fit into the song well enough to be used almost by himself on the twelve-inch single's dub side, "Not So Far Away." Hancock had started the session warming up to the vocal version's chord changes and ended up blowing

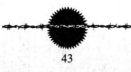

Bono. *(Photo: Kristen Stetler)*

Back, l-r: Big Youth, Lou Reed, Reuben Blades, John Oates, and Little Steven; front, l-r: Danny Schecter; Video Director, Jonathan Demme; and Video Producer Hart Perry. *(Photo: David Seelig/Star File)*

L-r: Lottie Golden, Tina B, and B.J. Nelson, members of BLT. *(Photo: Reuven Kopitchinski)*

Front, l-r: Scorpio, Fat Boys, Little Steven, and B.J. Nelson at the East Harlem video shoot. *(Photo: Reuven Kopitchinski)*

everybody's mind with a seven-minute solo. He then left through the chaos of news crews and documentary makers who had been hanging around the studio in increasing numbers as the word got out. Baker, ecstatic, saw Steven looking a bit preoccupied. "What's the matter?" he bravely asked, having gotten used to that look. "That was great, but it ain't gonna work with Miles, and the Miles stuff has got to be used." Hancock, after all, plays dance music as much as jazz these days, if such conventional terms can still be applied to the fringes of experimentation where records like "Rockit" are created.

The Davis tracks needed a different kind of support. Fortunately, Hancock was returning to New York a few weeks later to perform at the Village Gate with bassist Ron Carter and drummer Tony Williams, the other members of the fabled mid-60s Miles Davis Quartet. Williams was in the process of recording an album of his own with producer Michael Cuscuna at M&I Recording, so the "Sun City" crew adjourned there, and Hancock, Williams, and Carter overdubbed their parts atop that of the man who'd originally brought them together. Keyboardist Richard Scher (one of "Sun City's" constant presences) and the current king of Nigerian pop, drummer Sonny Okusons, were already on the tape, so the producers thought they were finished. A friend of Steven's had brought his three-year-old son to the sessions, and as the musicians were leaving Steven thought he'd get his opinion. "Well, Sam, what do you think?" "It needs some guitar," Sam replied deadpan. The brilliant young guitarist Stanley Jordan was added the next day.

In the meantime, yet another reclusive artist, Peter Gabriel, had been tracked down. A tape had been sent to Gabriel through his label in England, Charisma. Two weeks later, Gail Colson, Gabriel's manager, called Rick Dutka and offered to

Afrika Bambaataa. *(Photo: Harold Sinclair)*

Joey Ramone. *(Photo: Reuven Kopitchinski)*

L-r: John Oates, Lou Reed, and Ruben Blades. *(Photo: Reuven Kopitchinski)*

Melle Mel and Duke Bootee. *(Photo: Reuven Kopitchinski)*

Zöe Yanakis. *(Photo: Reuven Kopitchinski)*

Scorpio. *(Photo: Reuven Kopitchinski)*

donate "Biko" to what was fast becoming the *Sun City* LP. Since the "Sun City" crew wanted all new material, Dutka declined but pressed for Gabriel to make an appearance on *Sun City*. As it turned out, Gabriel was recording in New York the next week but never received the numerous phone messages Dutka left for him. Finally, Arthur Baker picked up the phone himself, called the Power Station studio where Gabriel was working (and where Baker was well known) and demanded to be put through. Gabriel took the call and readily agreed to participate in making *Sun City*. In fact, Gabriel agreed to come over and do the track that night.

"We didn't know exactly what we wanted him to do," Baker says. "So we gave him just the drums and the log drums in his headphones—the same as we had with Miles. He just sang to the drums. We were kind of looking for a chant, and he came up with his own lines.

"He just said, 'Well, let me go in and let me warm up a bit,' and that ["No More Apartheid"] is what he did," recalls Little Steven. "It was so incredible. He just did more and more until we ended up with five tracks of vocals. After a while, he just began to double certain riffs; he created the thing out of the air.

"I loved it, and it didn't really fit anywhere, of course. So I wanted to make it into its own song. Coincidentally, Tom Lord-Alge, one of the engineers, turned out to be a Peter Gabriel fanatic. So Tom and his equally crazed brother Chris took the track and had [percussionist and mix-master] Keith LeBlanc play some drums on it. We then brought Robbie Kilgore in on keyboards and just created music around what Peter had done." Arthur Baker says that LeBlanc created his effects by playing to the drum track alone and never heard Gabriel's vocal. Yet he achieved his remarkably sympathetic playing in only two takes. Later, parts were added by Van

Zandt on guitar, Zöe Yanakis on keyboards, and Doug Wimbish on bass.

Everyone in New York loved the result, but by this time Peter Gabriel had returned to England and had no idea of what they'd done with his work. "I was a little nervous about sending it to him, because it had gone through quite an evolution," Little Steven says. "But he loved it. He just suggested that we find Shankar, who he had worked with before." Shankar did come in and quickly added a beautiful part played on double violin, which combines characteristics of violin and cello.

Suddenly, there were enough versions of "Sun City"—or at least, expansions of its basic rhythm patterns—to make not only a single but an entire album.

Not every artist who Van Zandt and Baker approached was available. But one artist never had the option: he was in jail. From the begining Little Steven wanted the outspoken Nigerian superstar Fela Anikwapo Kuti, the creator of "afro-beat," on the record. But Fela was in jail for five years on a currency law infraction, a sentence his supporters say is trumped up and unfair.

So the "Sun City" project sent a cable to the head of Nigeria's military government asking for Fela to be released in order to take part in the project. Since Nigeria has been outspoken in its condemnations of apartheid, it was thought that he just might be released. No such luck. Instead, after Fela's manager Pascal Imbert flew to Lagos and read the appeal from the "Sun City" record project aloud during a press conference, Imbert was jailed too—although he was soon released. The whole flap was given prominent attention in the Nigerian press but went unreported in the United States.

Within weeks General Buhari, the Nigerian leader to whom the appeal was directed, was overthrown. Another Nigerian artist who later joined the record, Sonny Okosuns, carried a second appeal to Lagos but it proved ineffective as well. Ultimately this gesture of solidarity within a solidarity project couldn't do much more than draw some attention to Fela's plight.

In all, Artists United Against Apartheid, as the crew had decided to call itself, now had five tracks: two mixes of "Sun City," one featuring keyboards and synthesizers, the other guitars; "Let Me See Your I.D.," with Gil Scott-Heron providing narrative continuity for the rappers, who in the end included Peter Wolf, Melle Mel, Duke Bootee, Kurtis Blow, Sonny Okosuns, Scorpio, the Fat Boys, Jimmy Cliff, and South African exiles the Malopoets; "No More Apartheid," featuring Peter Gabriel and Shankar; "The Struggle Continues," featuring Miles Davis's technologically reunited quartet; and "Revolutionary Situation," a documentary montage which was compiled by Keith LeBlanc in the style of his Malcolm X homage, "No Sell Out," and by "The News Dissector" Danny Schechter, after the fashion of his old WBCN broadcasts.

"Revolutionary Situation" is an expecially fascinating part of the "Sun City" project because it features the voices of so many key players in the anti-apartheid struggle—including South African Prime Minister P.W. Botha, Ronald Reagan, Bishop Desmond Tutu, various voices recorded at rallies and funerals in South Africa, and, most startling of all, the voice of imprisoned African National Congress leader, Nelson Mandela.

Because Mandela has been imprisoned since 1964, most South Africans have never heard him speak, even though he is perhaps the greatest symbol of aspirations for black liberation. Schechter managed to locate in London an extremely rare tape of Mandela made in 1961, and it is intercut with his statements from prison read by one of his daughters. "It is useless and futile for us to continue talking

SILENCING THE OPPOSITION

The government can ban anyone it wishes to silence. Individuals who are banned are restricted to a particular area or placed under house arrest. They cannot be published or quoted and can meet with only one person at a time. They are prohibited from seeking employment and attending church or any other group activity. People such as Winnie Mandela, opponent of the regime and wife of political prisoner Nelson Mandela, and others, black and white, remain banned."

The Washington Office on Africa Educational Fund

(Opposite) In South Africa, funerals provide one of the few opportunities to protest government policies and police violence. In April 1985, tens of thousands of mourners buried twenty-seven people shot dead by the police. The state of emergency declared in July 1985 has severely restricted even this form of expression. *(Photo: Reuters/Bettman Newsphotos)*

peace and nonviolence against a government whose reply is only savage attacks," Nelson Mandela says. His comments are intercut with an introduction by his daughter and the freedom cry of "Amandla." It was also intercut with Miles Davis's hoarse rasp—"You can't go in there," he half whispers. "You're the wrong color." Amidst the ravings of the genuinely fanatical politicians like Reagan and Botha, Mandela's words seem inexorably logical, as if even a quarter century ago he had the ability to cut through all of apartheid's Orwellian jargon and obfuscation to express the simple truth of the matter.

By the time it was released, "Revolutionary Situation" seemed particularly fitting because, in the course of the "Sun City" recording project, the situation in South Africa had accelerated to its greatest crisis ever. The cycle of black insurrections that broke out around the time of Van Zandt's 1984 trips continued to grow throughout the spring and summer of 1985, and so did the chorus of calls for international—particularly American—firms to "disinvest" from South Africa. The college campus strikes were but one manifestation of the disinvestment movement and were designed to pressure university trustees into selling off their stock holdings in firms that do business in South Africa. (An important evolution of those strikes, "The Pledge for Equality in South Africa" has students signing a pledge not to work for companies doing business with South Africa until there is an end to apartheid.)

By midsummer, continuous unrest made disinvestment appear a wise strategy to many investors, though now most likely for purely economic reasons. As a result, the rand—South Africa's basic unit of currency—lost two-thirds of its value. Yet Prime Minister Botha remained unwavering in his commitment to cosmetic changes (but no real ones) in apartheid policies, thereby infuriating both his country's business community, which desperately needed to recapture foreign investment, as well as the right wing of his own political party, which split off in fury that even lip-service concessions had been made. Meanwhile, back in the United States, the Reagan Administration was forced to make a few cosmetic concessions of its own, instituting some mild sanctions against South Africa in order to prevent Congress from enacting far harsher ones.

In July of 1985, Botha declared a national state of emergency, giving the police even more sweeping authority than usual. But the increasingly militarized atmosphere hardly helped settle the situation, and on November 1, Pretoria announced complete censorship of all international press coverage of the racial warfare in South African streets. Apartheid had not yet reached its terminal crisis, but it seemed to be building in intensity each day.

*S*un City was created against this special backdrop, which intensified the interest and commitment of musicians to the project. However, in both America and England, where most of the major recording companies in the world are located, the issue of South Africa remained a testy question at the corporate level. Although individual artists were virtually willing to stand in line in order to participate, most record labels were considerably more reluctant.

Even while they were still in the process of making lists of whom to contact, Arthur Baker had played the "Sun City" demo for his friends at Tommy Boy Records, which had released most of his early work. The label's VP, Rick Dutka, had been particularly enthusiastic about the project, and it tied in with his own plans for the upcoming New Music Seminar, an annual international music industry gathering promoted by Tommy Boy's owner, Tom Silverman. Dutka planned to make the highlight of

Grandmaster Melle Mel. *(Photo: Loren Haynes)*

Miles Davis. *(Photo: David Seelig/Star File)*

Kashif. *(Photo: David Seelig/Star File)*

Bruce Springsteen. *(Photo: David Seelig/Star File)*

Little Steven and Peter Gabriel. *(Photo: David Seelig/Star File)*

L-r: Arthur Baker, Jimmy Cliff, and Little Steven. *(Photo: David Seelig/Star File)*

Arthur Baker, Shankar, and Bono. *(Photo: David Seelig/Star File)*

the 1985 Seminar a keynote speech and panel discussion about apartheid and the music industry. It would be a forum in which the realities of apartheid could be brought home to the music community and one in which anti-apartheid strategies could be discussed, providing artists and industry execs with a chance to speak out on an issue that had become increasingly important within an ever more internationalized record business. In the end, Dutka became the fourth member of the "Sun City" crew, initially assisting in locating artists and participating in discussions of who would do the actual distribution of the record, which still had no home.

One of the things that homelessness meant to "Sun City" was a limit on how much money the Artists United Against Apartheid organizers could spend, even for essentials. All the studio time—at various locations in New York, London, and Los Angeles—was donated. Van Zandt's double round-trip airfare to London came out of his own pocket. David Seelig had been shooting stills, and Hart Perry was filming the studio sessions for no money at all.

As *Sun City* headed toward completion, it became self-evident that Shakedown Sound would be inadequate for mixing such a massive and complex record. Only a few studios in the States—let alone in New York City—had the kind of computerized mixing console (which can monitor not only what tracks are being used but also the settings and minor adjustments that go along with them) that was indispensable to take those 300-plus tracks spread out over 13 master tapes and boil them down to a half-inch reel ready to be mastered and made into records and cassettes.

Attorney Owen Epstein entered the picture, both to help negotiate the recording company contract and to work on obtaining clearances to use various artists from the record labels to which they were regularly

contracted. The latter task was unbelievably time-consuming all by itself—and without getting a label deal, all that paperwork would have been meaningless. And this deal was not easy to make. Even for a project with the combined clout of its many stars, Artists United Against Apartheid had certain fundamental needs that were quite unusual, in terms of both creative control and record company commitments.

The "Sun City" organizers recognized that the importance of the consciousness-raising aspect of the project was even greater than the fund-raising side. Realizing that large corporations subsist only by making a profit from their activities, Artists United Against Apartheid agreed that any label that eventually released the record would not be required to devote all *its* revenues from *Sun City* sales to the cause of South African freedom. (It would be sufficient that the artists donated their royalties.) It was more important to find a label that not only empathized with the project but could also deliver when it came to getting the disc to the stores and onto the airwaves. That kind of commitment from the record label would require some heavy cash outlay—not only to help defray the costs of the sessions, but also, for instance, to pay for a video and to hire extra promotion people. And it would also mean temporarily distracting that label's own staff members from other ongoing projects. The "Sun City" project also insisted that an information sheet about apartheid be included as well as a full-color insert, including lyrics and photos. This would ensure that the very special audience that bought the record would be able to share in the experience of making it.

Not every label was interested, and of those who were supportive, not all could meet "Sun City"'s needs. For instance, although Dutka was intimately involved in the record and even though Tom Silverman was also an enthusiast of the idea, Tommy Boy

was never a real possibility because it lacked the world-wide distribution of a major label. Neither did it have the clout to get a potentially controversial record on the air.

And *Sun City was* potentially controversial: It might have been treated as "just another charity record" by some, this time an attempt to do some fund-raising for the cause of fighting racism rather than famine. But once people heard it, they understood that Van Zandt and his cohorts had created something far different, a record that took a stand on a tremendously controversial topic. Although *Sun City*'s lyrics did not mention violators of the boycott by name, it made its attitude toward Ronald Reagan's approach unmistakable, giving the line, "This quiet diplomacy ain't nothin' but a joke" to Darlene Love, one of the most spectacular voices in the ensemble.

At one point, the team was so concerned that no major record label would commit itself to the project that the idea of forming their own label, Solidarity Records, was seriously considered. In fact, Baker says, they had decided to release the record on Solidarity no matter who they signed with—until Bruce Lundvall of Manhattan Records entered the picture.

Lundvall seemed perfect for the project, both personally and professionally. A devoted jazz fan, he had recently presided over the successful relaunching of Blue Note Records, and he was eager to establish Manhattan's reputation. As President at Elektra Records, Lundvall had signed Ruben Blades and taken several other interesting artistic chances, but he was no mere avant-gardist; his chief experience was as more than a decade at CBS Records, culminating in the Presidency of one of the most successful record companies in America. Manhattan was Lundvall's own label, but it was supported by the marketing clout and promotional capital of Capitol/EMI, a well-endowed record business conglomerate. By early September, a deal was finalized for Manhattan to release *Sun City*, with artists' royalties being donated to The Africa Fund.

Early on, the "Sun City" project decided that, unlike Bob Geldof or the folks who organized USA for Africa, they would not be able to form and run their own charity. Instead they decided to turn over the money to The Africa Fund, a highly respected charitable trust affiliated with the American Committee on Africa and with more than twenty-five years of experience in supporting Africa's quest for freedom. The tax-exempt group agreed to accept royalties to be earmarked to meet three needs: political prisoners and their families inside South Africa; educational and cultural programs for South Africa; educational and cultural programs for South Africans forced into exile; and the educational programs of the anti-apartheid groups, the American Committee on Africa and TransAfrica.

The New Music Seminar panel on apartheid was scheduled for Friday, September 27. Little Steven would be one of the panelists, along with the United Nations representative of the African National Congress, Neo Mnumzana, South African musician Sipho "Hot Stix" Mabuse, exiled poet and boycott organizer Dennis Brutus, longtime activist Elombe Brath, musician Jerry Dammers (composer of the U.K. hit "Free Nelson Mandela"), and Stevie Wonder's manager, Abner. (Wonder worked steadily against apartheid throughout 1985 and was among those arrested for demonstrating outside the South African embassy in Washington D.C. His presence on *Sun City* would have been more than welcome, but the organizers' several approaches to him [they never reached him on the phone] were not pursued after it was learned that one of the centerpieces of *In Square Circle*, Wonder's first album in five years, was a song called "It's Wrong (Apartheid)." Clearly, Stevie was already doing his bit for freedom.)

Not only was the apartheid panel an impressive

Pat Benatar. *(Photo: Loren Haynes)*

MEDICAL CARE

"There is one doctor for every 330 whites, 730 Indians, 1,200 Coloureds and 12,000 Africans. In the homelands there is one doctor for every 14,000 people in Transkei, 17,000 in Bophuthatswana and 19,000 in Gazankulu. These figures are said to be comparable to those for the most underdeveloped countries in the world."

The Apartheid Handbook, *Roger Omond, Penguin Books*

- Infant mortality rates for rural blacks are thirty-one times higher than for whites.
- In the rural bantustans one-half of the black children die before age five.
- The black township of Soweto has only one hospital for an estimated two million blacks.

The Washington Office on Africa Educational Fund

The city water supply in Bophuthatswana: In many of the homelands the water is contaminated, contributing significantly to the serious diseases which afflict and kill South Africans; sometimes the only way to get "pure" water is to purchase it from the local authorities. *(Photo: The Africa Fund)*

gathering, but the New Music Seminar was attended annually by more than 5,000 people, including many of the college broadcasters, rock journalists, and other tradespeople who could do the most to support *Sun City* at the outset. (Everyone involved was well aware that as far as hit-oriented radio was concerned, a record either had it in the grooves or it didn't. The fact that a significant political issue was concerned was not going to get *Sun City* on the pop airwaves—in fact, it might even prove a drawback, all the more reason to make the music irresistible.) So it was decided that the Seminar would be a perfect launching pad for the record, and Baker and Van Zandt began working on the mixes with that goal in mind.

Before they could even begin to think about mixing the record, though, someone had to sit down with all of the tapes and pick out the individual lines that fit together best. "The questions that needed to be answered were: Who follows who? What little stretch of the melody works well with this?" Van Zandt says. "It got really complicated, because almost nobody sang the actual melody of the song— they got close sometimes. I basically wrote it keeping what was about to happen in mind. I kept the melody flexible enough for everyone to get their own personalities in, and it worked, but it was still a lot of decisions in the end. And there were a few cases—Bobby Womack, Darlene Love—where every line was so good, you wanted to keep 'em all."

In any event, it took about two weeks in early September merely to sort out what they wanted to keep. And it was only then, when those dozens of tidbits could be assembled in one room, that the task of mixing them into a single coherent record began.

That required an SSL computer-equipped board, which meant that Baker and Van Zandt had to go looking for some generous or committed studio to donate one. As it turned out they were able to work

for free in several places, notably New York's Hit Factory and Electric Ladyland, but for a time it seemed as if they would have to leave for Nashville or Miami in order to do the mixes.

Two days before the New Music Seminar's apartheid panel, they realized that they'd never be finished in time—which meant not only that the record would miss being heard by the NMS audience, but also that they'd have to push back its release date. The single, which had been scheduled for early October release to radio and record stores, was now scheduled for a middle- to late-October issue date. Even with the extra time, Van Zandt and Baker still had to keep cracking the whip over themselves, because the mixing wasn't the only loose end in the project. There were an album cover to design, credit sheets to write and approve, an MTV "Liner Notes" special to create (which would be shown in lieu of the record at the apartheid panel, where it received a standing ovation), and of course, *Sun City*'s own video to organize and complete.

The original hope had been to do videos of all the album tracks; and several well-known directors, including Richard Attenbrough, Jonathan Demme, Alan J. Pakula, and Milos Forman had expressed interest in working with the project. The long-form idea was later postponed, but there remained an immediate need for a conventional MTV-style video clip; several experienced directors volunteered, among them Demme and the British team of Kevin Godley and Lol Creme, who are among the most technically innovative in the field. Godley and Creme accepted the assignment, but it turned out that the date of the New York shooting— October 10 and 11, the weekend of a major anti-apartheid rally there—conflicted with earlier commitments they'd made in London. In order for the video

Front, l-r: Via Afrika, David Ruffin, and Jimmy Cliff in Washington Square Park. *(Photo: Reuven Kopitchinski)*

Front, l-r: David Ruffin, Via Afrika, and Eddie Kendrick. *(Photo: David Seelig/Star File)*

L-r: Darlene Love, Run-DMC, Little Steven, and Arthur Baker. *(Photo: David Seelig/Star File)*

to be finished to coincide with the album's release, the shooting could not be postponed. Demme generously stepped in and directed the filming, assisted by Hart Perry and Niles Siegel. The shoots took place at several locations throughout Manhattan on Thursday and in midtown at the Citicorp center at the anti-apartheid rally on Friday afternoon.

Invitations were sent out to everyone who had appeared in the *Sun City* sessions. The shoot would start Thursday afternoon at various locations around town—East Harlem for the rappers, Hell's Kitchen for Springsteen, Kendrick and Ruffin, Blades, John Oates, and Lou Reed, the East Village for Bono, Darlene Love, Joey Ramone, Peter Wolf, Jimmy Cliff, Nona Hendryx, and Kashif—followed by a dinner for the entire cast at a midtown hotel (where the various out-of-towners were staying), then a night shoot at Washington Square Park.

Most of those who attended the video shooting were already based in New York. A few, like Boston's Peter Wolf, flew in from cities nearby. (Some shooting was done on the West Coast, to incorporate Dylan and Browne, for instance; and most of the California and London sessions had already been filmed.) The performer who traveled furthest to make the video was Bono, of the Irish group U2. Bono had recorded on his own in Dublin, just before leaving for six weeks at a feeding camp in Ethiopia. He returned from Ethiopia, stopped in Dublin to gather a few belongings, and then immediately flew off to New York for the video. When he arrived he bore a Christlike beard on his chin and a soulfully glazed cast in his eye—the product of natural inclinations, what he'd seen in Ethiopia, and not having slept for the better part of a week.

In East Harlem, kids were so excited to see their rap heroes Bambaataa, Melle Mel, Run-DMC, Blow, and the rest gathered all in one place, and the crew was so unprepared to deal with such intrusions, that

Malopoets and Little Steven. *(Photo: David Seelig/Star File)*

L-r: Stiv Bator, Michael Monroe, and Joey Ramone. *(Photo: David Seelig/Star File)*

L-r: Ron Carter, Herbie Hancock, and Tony Williams. *(Photo: Lisa Podgur)*

"I knew of Steve's involvement during the past couple of years, and that he'd been down [to South Africa] and back a couple of times. I don't think I could just sit back and watch what was going on without feeling that I had to say something about it. The funny thing about it is that [apartheid] is so out in the open down there, but I was hoping that by helping bring attention to what's going on in South Africa it'd also make us look in our own backyards, at the terrible problems we have with racism right here in this country right now. So when Steve said, 'Come on!' I said, 'Sure!' The record sounds great —it's a great rock record that's going to be powerful because it's just great music. For me, music was always informative, educational, and fun, and I think that's what this record is."

—Bruce Springsteen

"Steven told me he'd break my arms and legs if I turned him down! [Laughs.] No, he rang me up at home right at the beginning of the project and said, 'Do you want to be on the record?' And I just said, 'Yes.' It was very easy—one word."

—Bono (U2)

the crowd became a part of the shoot. Ultimately, they had to use the earliest takes, because the crowd was all but drowning out the rappers by doubling their lines in the final shots. The Fat Boys added to the drama by showing up late (and finally not making the East Harlem shots at all). "We'd keep getting updates," says one of the principals. " 'They've left the Deli on 78th Street and they're up to the hot dog stand on 86th.... O.K., they'd been spotted at the Burger King at 96th.' It was hilarious—and perfect." In Hell's Kitchen the shooting proceeded without a hitch and was on schedule when it came time to repair to the hotel for dinner.

Bono had arrived, but he was thoroughly exhausted and went upstairs to his room to sleep for a bit. In the meantime, everyone else adjourned to the dining room. "That was the first time everybody really realized what was happening," Van Zandt says. "You gotta picture artists coming in from all over the world, nobody really knowing who else was on it. Nobody ever really knew whether the record was gonna *come out*. It was really funny at the dinner— you could see people going: 'God, he's on it, too!'

"You know, artists don't get a chance to see each other and talk to each other...ever—which people don't know. What was great about this evening was that everyone *did* get a chance to meet and talk and realize that this very spontaneous vision had actually been realized."

That spirit sustained the ensemble as it headed south to Washington Square Park in the heart of Greenwich Village, still the center of Manhattan's youth scene. There was only one problem: Even though they had a perfectly valid permit to shoot in the park that night, no one had bothered to tell the local cops that there were so many performers involved—and, especially, nobody had bothered to tell them that Bruce Springsteen, one of the two or three biggest stars in the world, was among them.

The local precinct had sent down three or four cops, but when the officers there saw what was going on, they called for back-up. Soon, the park was cordoned off by what Dutka described as "the riot squad without their riot gear."

Of course, this only increased the attraction to passersby, who now surrounded the scene so heavily that the police ultimately relegated the crew to shooting in the park's central fountain, preventing the crowd from mixing with the artists—which was the reason for shooting in Washington Square in the first place. (Not that the cops were successful in keeping the stars from the fans anyway. Bono couldn't keep himself from the onlookers and went over to chat, which is just what the police had hoped to prevent.)

Nevertheless, the group shots taken that night are marvelously reflective of the collective energy and enthusiasm that filled the air—as if coming together in such a large body had surprised each artist into a new understanding of the creative spirit behind "Sun City," into a deepened awareness of what Artists United Against Apartheid actually meant. You could see it in the sparks that flew as Peter Wolf kicked up his heels, as Duke Bootee flung his finger into the lens and Melle Mel twirled his hat in the air, as even Arthur Baker shook it on down and Bono snatched up a Fat Boy and line-danced him past the cameras, planting a huge kiss on his cheek as they cruised on by.

The shoot completed, almost everyone went home to prepare for the next afternoon's filming at the anti-apartheid rally uptown. The exceptions were Baker and Van Zandt—who had to return to the studio to complete the final mixes, which were due to be mastered Monday morning—and Bono and Wolf, who decided to visit the Rolling Stones in Right Track, the West Side studio where they were recording their album. Bono still needed a lot of sleep, but according to Little Steven, "He was

L-r: Zak Starkey, Little Steven, and Ringo Starr. *(Photo: Barbara Bach))*

Front, l-r: Owen Epstein, Little Steven, and Arthur Baker; back, l-r: Doug Wimbish and Keith LeBlanc.
(Photo: David Seelig/Star File)

THE INTERNAL SECURITY ACT OF 1982

"This act allows:

1) indefinite incommunicado detention without charge or trial
2) the outlawing of any organization alleged to be threatening to public safety or order
3) the prohibition of the printing, publication, or dissemination of any periodical or. . .other publication
4) the prohibition of any gathering or meeting
5) random police searches
6) the curtailment of travel rights of any person, and restriction of rights of communication, association and participation in any activity (banning).

Further it is illegal under this act to render any assistance to any campaign, at home or abroad, that protests or seeks to modify or repeal any laws as such a campaign furthers the aims of a banned organization."

South Africa Fact Sheet, *January 1984, The Africa Fund*

Thousands of South African troops lined the streets of Sebokeng township in October 1984 while the police conducted a house-to-house search resulting in 349 arrests for a variety of offenses. *(Photo: UPI/Bettman Newsphotos)*

DETENTION

"...they would come in the middle of the night....You just heard someone interfering with your neck, they came with a wire. He says, 'I'm going to strangle you, because you don't want to tell the truth or tell me about other people. I will tell the whole world that you've committed suicide. Then he'd walk out.'"

Khosi Mbatha, at a press conference in London in November 1982, speaking about her detention

"For the first fifty-six days of my detention I changed from a mainly vertical to a mainly horizontal creature. A black iron bedstead became my world....Left in that cell long enough I feared to become one of those colourless insects that slither under a world of flat grey stones away from the sky and sunlight, the grass and people."

117 Days, Ruth First, Penguin (Ruth First, a white South African journalist, was killed in her university office in Mozambique by a book bomb believed to have been sent by the South African police.)

(Opposite) Violence, resulting in death, can come at any time in South Africa. *(Photo: Reuters/Bettman Newsphotos)*

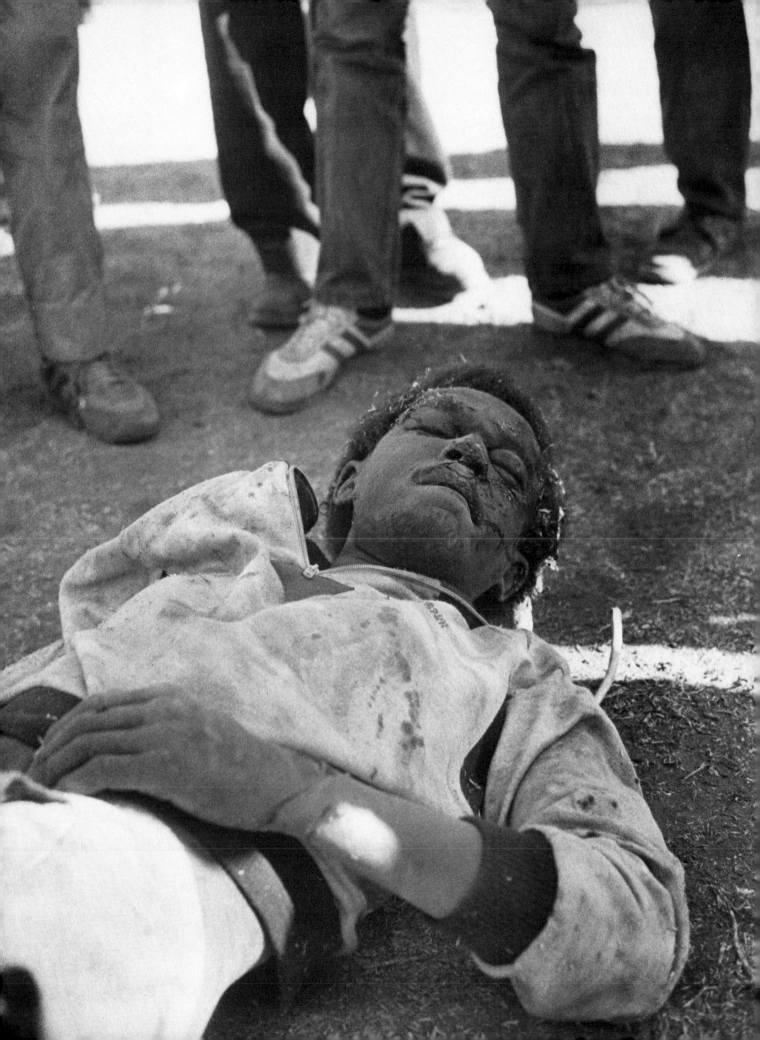

beyond sleep, and I know that feeling quite well. He had the intensity of a man who has known greatness and is called upon one last time to contribute to life before leaving the earth." So he and Wolf adjourned.

Somewhere along the line that night, they ended up talking about the blues. Bono had never listened to much of that kind of music; he'd once said that U2 was formed as a reaction against the kind of traditional bands they'd heard in Ireland. Wolf, on the other hand, was a great connoisseur of blues and R&B—virtually a patron of Muddy Waters, James Cotton, and other blues giants, putting them up in his house when they traveled to Boston, chauffeuring them around, making sure that many of them got decent money as the opening act for his J. Geils Band, studying the music and basing his act and persona on the tradition they'd founded.

Keith Richards and Ron Wood of the Stones, of course, were equally passionate on the subject. As it transpired that night, Bono had never heard the real stuff. When he did—as tapes of old country blues masters like Son House and Robert Johnson were played—his eyes were opened.

They didn't get back to the hotel until after dawn, but early that afternoon, still short on sleep, Bono asked that Arthur Baker find a guitar and have it sent to his hotel room, saying that he had a couple of songs he wanted to write. That evening he and Wolf againt went over to the Stones sessions, but when Bono returned he found the guitar waiting for him, and he stayed up into the morning hours, writing his songs.

"After the shoot Thursday night, Steven and I spoke with the head cop on duty at the park," Dutka recalls. "He said he thought everything went well, and we encouraged him to say so to his bosses at the precinct. But the next day, the mayor's office called to say that they were revoking our permit to shoot anywhere in the city—especially at the Citicorp building. The reason turned out to be that the cops simply didn't expect what happened the night before, and they didn't want to risk a repeat. There were about two hours of really heavy scrambling before we convinced them that we did have sufficient security to handle the situation—that this was a group of artists that was well under control.

"And it really was. What happened during the shooting at the mass rally against apartheid was really unusual. That day was an international day of protest against South Africa, and so the demonstration at the Citicorp building was part of a much larger spirit. The American Committee on Africa and District 65 of the UAW had organized it, and there were about 3,000 people out there. They completely filled the block on Fifty-fourth Street between Third Avenue and Lexington Avenue.

"It was an incredible sight, and it was even more incredible to see these artists gathered there to take a stand *visibly.* But what was even better was that, unlike the night before when the cops were able to separate the stars from the masses, this time there were only a few wooden horses between them. So these artists became very visibly one with the cause. When the filming started, we got the whole crowd singing and raising their fists, chanting 'I...I....I/ Ain't gonna play Sun City.' It was like an electric charge sent throughout the crowd. What was a good demonstration became an exciting event."

The day's events ended, after an impromptu get-together between the artists and Rev. Jesse Jackson (who had spoken at the rally), in a rare spirit of creative and political unity.

In the meantime, Baker and Little Steven were trying to complete the mixes. At nine Saturday evening, Bono turned up at the studio, saying he wanted to record one of his new songs, "Silver and Gold." The title was apparently inspired by the fact that the

Nona Hendryx. *(Photo: Jobi Carnes)*

David Ruffin and Eddie Kendrick. *(Photo: David Seelig/Star File)*

Jackson Browne. *(Photo: Shelly Ross)*

Daryl Hall. *(Photo: David Seelig/Star File)*

economy of South Africa (the world's largest producer of gold and diamonds) is principally based on
mining such precious metals and that almost all of
the dirty and dangerous work of mining is done by
blacks, at what amounts to slave wages.

But the lyrics to "Silver and Gold" are more
elliptical than any description can serve, and Bono's
performance, which initially featured just himself
and his acoustic guitar with a heavy foot stomp,
amounts to a meditative conversation with his own
soul about the spiritual consequences of living in
such a world. Filled with gutteral asides, occasional
whoops, and half-muttered incoherencies, "Silver
and Gold" is a transcendent, contemporary communication of the exorcism of the same hell hounds that
plagued the great blues innovator, Robert Johnson,
fifty years ago. But today's demons have names.

Bono had already said that he wanted Keith
Richards to record a guitar part for the song. While
they waited to get in touch with the Stones, Keith
LeBlanc, who happened to be in the studio, overdubbed a percussion part by banging on a cardboard
freight box, which added to the song's primitive
atmosphere while giving the music some of the drive
of a kick drum. Time was getting late, and the mixing had come to a standstill while they waited to finish the Bono track. The entire album cover and
credits were already at the printer, and there was no
way that Bono's song could even be listed on the
sleeve—but there was also no doubt on anyone's part
that he had just come up with a perfect conclusion to
the album, something that brought the music back to
its roots and the topic back to its most basic
emotion.

So Peter Wolf was recruited to track down the
Stones. As it developed, the Stones were so deep
into studio time that Keith Richards didn't even rise
from bed until 2 AM. Finally, at 5 AM, the "Sun

City" crew—Baker, Little Steven, Zöe Yanakis, Tina
B, engineer Tom Lord-Alge, and Bono—went to
Right Track to meet with the Stones.

The scene at Right Track was "a classic Stones
session," says Baker. Dawn was already approach-
ing, but first the social amenities had to be observed,
and everyone adjourned to a listening room to hear
seven completed tracks from the new Stones album.
Meanwhile, *New York Times* critic Robert Palmer
and some others were in the studio, Palmer playing
his clarinet along with the Stones tracks. Also with
the Stones that night were producer Steve Lilywhite
and the Stones engineer Dave Jordan, "plus about a
dozen assistants."

By 7:00 Sunday morning, Keith and compatriot
Ron Wood had heard the basic "Silver and Gold"
track and had agreed to become part of Artists
United Against Apartheid by playing on it. Working
alongside them were Palmer on clarinet and percussionist Steve Jordan on yet another freight box. Four
women, led by Tina B, added a chorus. Bono also
attempted to redo his vocal several times, but the
original performance was too special—there was no
way to match it. After three or four takes, the Stones
and company had added their parts; "Silver and
Gold" was wrapped. On Sunday afternoon, October
12, a little more than a year after Little Steven Van
Zandt left South Africa for the last time, the recording of *Sun City* was finally finished.

"The weirder part of the story is that we didn't
all just go on home," says Baker. "We couldn't.
Bono had to get ready to go back to Ireland, and
Steve and I were still supposed to master on Monday.
So we sent Steve home to sleep for a while, and Tom
and I went to mix "Silver and Gold" and finish a
couple of other tracks."

They headed for the Power Station, their third
studio in less than twenty-four hours, but when they
arrived the tape machine's heads needed to be

aligned, a time-consuming process. Baker decided to go home and get some sleep instead of waiting up. He awoke the next morning, expecting to go to the studio, but found that Bono and Tom Lord-Alge had stayed up all night mixing. Steven came in after a few hours sleep and looked into the desperate, fanatical, adrenaline-shot eyes of Bono and Tom and declared their mix perfect. Bono couldn't quite believe it and said, "Look, I gotta leave the room. Make whatever changes it needs and I'll listen again." Steven smiled at Tom who by this time resembled the eccentric inventor who knows he's got the right formula. Tom smiled insanely back and Steven made a few minor changes. Bono came back and loved it and suddenly they were done. The tapes were taken to Bob Ludwig at Masterdisk that morning to begin the mastering process. *Sun City*—that "spontaneous vision"—was finally a reality.

Of course, a record's life doesn't end when it finally reaches vinyl. That's just when it truly begins to take shape, a shape which is determined by who hears it and what happens when they do. In that sense, the story of *Sun City* and Artists United Against Apartheid has barely begun, and what's been told here is mere prologue.

But even in the first few weeks after the record's release, it was obvious that some quick lessons had been learned—most of all, by the artists themselves. They had proved that a political viewpoint could be articulated simply and directly and still make an exciting record. For instance, Joey Ramone summed up what everybody felt about conditions in South Africa, when he said, "I'll tell ya, it's disgusting!"

Even if *Sun City* had only served the purpose of making a few popular musicians intensely aware of apartheid and the struggle to end it, or if all the project had done was plug the international community of popular musicians into the right side of that

struggle, it could have been accounted a success. Amidst the community of those musicians—where freedom is too often confused with self-indulgent spectacle— *Sun City* sent a message of what freedom truly is.

Sun City, however, has gone beyond even this valuable lesson. The record's artistic success is equally unquestionable. If only by uniting such a diverse complement of performers, *Sun City* had made an effective statement. But what's even more interesting is that *Sun City* integrated all these musicians into a variety of recordings that were not only listenable but adventurous, at the cutting edge of contemporary popular styles, and at the same time, deeply and clearly rooted in musicial tradition.

Of course, *Sun City* aimed to do much more, and in the first few days after its release, it seemed that its goals would be easily reached, at least in the United States. (European release did not take place until after this book was completed.) In the urban Northeast, particularly in normally conservative New York, radio stations of almost every format immediately aired *Sun City* and talked about what it meant. Around the country it was usually the most adventurous programmers who played *Sun City* right away—but that's true of any new record, particularly of a new record whose *sound* is also new. *Sun City* was the product of a kind of dance-rock fusion that many American radio programmers haven't yet woken up to. Given those circumstances, *Sun City* looked like an immediate hit.

Thereafter the sledding got much tougher. There was resistance from radio programmers who thought that the record was "too political," as if popular music were required by law to stay away from subjects that touched the real world too closely. There were nonprogrammers who wanted it off the air, as well. In South Carolina, one station was told by the Ku Klux Klan that either *Sun City* came off the air

or the station and its personnel would face serious consequences. Quite naturally, the record came off the air. As this book went to press, the commercial fate of *Sun City* hung in the balance.

Yet none of these events really speaks to the most significant component of *Sun City,* its success as a political statement. How can this best be measured? Not only in the amount of records sold, or even in the number of pop stars moved to state—loudly and unequivocally—that they wouldn't be caught dead in Sun City, but also in the activity it stirs toward ending apartheid, and by that standard, *Sun City* is already a political success. By forcing the issue of racism, by inducing TV shows like *Entertainment Tonight* and MTV's "Liner Notes" to present a discussion of apartheid, *Sun City* does its job, whether or not it ever makes A-1 on the jukebox.

And perhaps it does its job just as effectively by being banished from the radio in South Carolina, or never making it to the airwaves at all in far too many American cities. This illustrates a point, as well. For *Sun City* attracted so many American musicians because they were all too aware that they, also, live in a racist society. Even politicians came out to back *Sun City.* On November 6, Los Angeles Mayor Tom Bradley held a reception honoring Little Steven, Jackson Browne, George Clinton, and Herbie Hancock. At the same time, he issued a statement calling South African apartheid an "evil system" and saying that it was the "obligation" of all radio stations to play *Sun City:* "I believe the people of this city do care, and I urge them to call their favorite radio station and request *Sun City.* I challenge local radio stations to play *Sun City* and help communicate this important message." Whether Bradley managed to make LA radio stations respond more dramatically to *Sun City* was finally less important than his own willingness to take a stand—and his ability, as the

L-r: Miles Davis, Little Steven, and Arthur Baker. *(Photo: David Seelig/Star File)*

Stanley Jordan and Arthur Baker. *(Photo: David Seelig/Star File)*

Miles Davis and Little Steven. *(Photo: David Seelig/Star File)*

THE PROPAGANDA

"That black South Africans are culturally, ethnically and politically fragmented into mutually-hostile tribes which are each being given separate nationhood in separate sovereign states for their own protection and for the accommodation of their separate cultural and political aspirations."

THE FACTS

"Unlike their counterparts in some countries of the north, South Africa's blacks do not have a tradition of tribal politics. For more than a century, no black political movement of significance has promoted or practised tribalism. Black South Africans have, on the contrary, long condemned tribalism as serving the 'divide and rule' policies imposed by whites. Tribalism is not easily accommodated within the sophisticated political thinking of urban blacks, and South African blacks have, in any case, in the relatively homogeneous Nguni culture (Xhosa—Zulu—Swazi—Ndebele) a lot in common."

Apartheid—the Propaganda and the Reality
by Donald Woods

A grave in the homeland of Bophuthatswana, where black South Africans who are considered members of the tribe Tswana, have been forcibily relocated. Instead of a headstone, the grave has been marked with the meager personal possessions this woman left behind. *(Photo: The Africa Fund)*

city's leading politician, to place those stations on the spot who were looking to duck potential controversy. This in turn helped establish what was wrong with America itself.

Little Steven perfectly articulated these feelings when he spoke at the apartheid panel of the New Music Seminar. Asked what he hoped the *Sun City* record would achieve, he listed several goals and then said, "Finally, I hope that by focusing on the exaggeration of racism [in South Africa], we can realize that racism is very much alive in our own country, and that we can begin to dismantle our own apartheid right here at home." Steven knew exactly to whom he was speaking, for sitting before him in the audience was Albert Turner, the Alabama civil rights activist who had just been indicted by the U.S. federal government for so-called "vote fraud."

What Van Zandt said had far deeper roots, ones he would recognize even if he didn't know them directly. "Something is happening in our world," Dr. Martin Luther King, Jr., once said. "The masses of people are rising up and wherever they are assembled today, whether they are in Johannesburg, South Africa; Nairobi, Kenya, Ghana; New York City; Atlanta, Georgia; Jackson, Mississippi; or Memphis, Tennessee, the cry is always the same: We want to be free." The first measure of *Sun City* is that it exactly lives up to the implications of Dr. King's statement.

But *Sun City's* success is finally much more concrete. After the United Nations ceremony, Danny Schechter, Rick Dutka, and a few others spent a few moments talking to E.S. Reddy, former director of the United Nations Committee on Apartheid. Mr. Reddy had participated in his first anti-apartheid demonstration in 1946, and he spoke about *Sun City* from the well of knowledge gained during those forty years of experience and frustration. "It is one thing to boycott South Africa," Mr. Reddy said. "But it is a tremendous thing to get these musicians and artists involved, because they reach people we never reach. The United Nations is symbolic, but to help people directly can do so much more."

In that sense, the story of Artists United Against Apartheid and *Sun City* has no ending—at least, not until Little Steven arrives in Johannesburg to finally play his song. On Independence Day, remember?

Afrika Bambaataa. *(Photo: Reuven Kopitchinski)*

L-r: Kurtis Blow, Jimmy Cliff, Ray Barretto, and Little Steven. *(Photo: David Seelig/Star File)*

Front: Bruce Springsteen and David Ruffin. *(Photo: Reuven Kopitchinski)*

Washington Square Park revelers. *(Photo: Reuven Kopitchinski)*

"For the last seventy-two years, blacks and Indians in South Africa have been told to be patient, and they've been patient long enough, I think. It's time they received equal opportunity. It's time for them to just run their own land, really, be it good or bad. Let them have a go at it."

—Kashif

"Every time I look at the papers, the problems have to do with man's inhumanity to man. We just haven't learned how to live together yet. We're going to have to get together somehow, or the human race won't be around much longer. We've developed too many ways that make it possible for almost any man on the street to wipe out the planet. This project is important because it emphasizes that learning to live together is our number one priority, and I wanted to be a part of that."

—Herbie Hancock

"The day American musicans will come to sing about apartheid in South Africa will be the day apartheid in South Africa will cease to exist."

—Sonny Okosuns

Making the video. *(Photo: Reuven Kopitchinski)*

L-r: Eddie Kendrick, Herbie Hancock, David Ruffin, and Arthur Baker. *(Photo: David Seelig/Star File)*

Afrika Bambaataa and Little Steven. *(Photo: David Seelig/Star File)*

Bonnie Raitt and Little Steven. *(Photo: David Seelig/Star File)*

John Oates and Little Steven. *(Photo: Reuven Kopitchinski)*

"What hurts is being driven like an animal out of your own home town. I was born in Johannesburg and proud of it. Now they tell me I'm a citizen of an up-country state called Qwa-Qwa—I've never ever seen the bloody place."

A taxi driver speaking to a reporter from the Sowetan *newspaper in February 1981*

THE ECONOMICS OF THE HOMELANDS

- Unemployment is said to be 27.5 percent among the economically active population.
- In 1980, 81 percent of the people lived below the poverty line.
- 13 percent of the population is classified as destitute, meaning they have no jobs, no pension payments, no land, and no cattle.
- 72 percent of the total gross national income of the homelands in 1980 was income earned by the migrant workers who travel to "white" South Africa.

The Apartheid Handbook, *Roger Omond, Penguin Books*

Bophuthatswana, one of the independent homelands which serves as a model of "successful" relocation and "improved" living conditions for black in South Africa, is in reality a poverty-stricken dumping ground for all those no longer wanted in white South Africa. *(Photo: The African Fund)*

LIFE IN THE HOSTELS

"There are about a dozen of them. These long narrow-built compartments accommodate 'single' men, i.e. migrant workers. In Soweto alone 60,000 men are hostel dwellers. Indoors, the inmates share the dormitories in tribal groups, as required by government law. In each dormitory are moveable black-painted iron and steel beds, a common one-plate coal stove and iron bar lockers used by the occupants. Barbed wire fences [separate] the hostel premises from [the surrounding residential areas]. There are no dining rooms, no visitors' rooms, no reading rooms, no recreation facilities, and absolutely no privacy for the inmates. Women are not allowed to venture into the hostel premises."

A Window on Soweto, *Joyce Sikakane,*
International Defence & Aid Fund, London, 1977

The hostels, which are more like prisons than residencies, are often the only places in which black South Africans can legally live and still remain fairly close to work. *(Photo: Danny Schechter)*

The Voices of *Sun City*

Afrika Bambaataa—Pioneering rapper and founder of the Zulu Nation, the socially minded youth gang from the Bronx, Bambaataa scored huge international successes with "Planet Rock" (which garnered him a gold record in the U.S.) and "Looking for the Perfect Beat" in the early 80s. More recently, Bam has collaborated with such diverse talents as James Brown and John Lydon.

Ray Barretto—The preeminent Latin New York percussionist is one of the fathers of modern salsa. A bandleader, he has also appeared as a guest player with a range of artists from Dizzy Gillespie to the Rolling Stones.

Stiv Bator—Former charter member of Cleveland's Dead Boys, Stiv is now singing with the Lords of the New Church.

Pat Benatar—Pat's involvement on *Sun City* is consistent with her outspokenness on a variety of personal issues, including child abuse. She has recently completed her seventh album, and she and her husband, guitarist/producer Neil Geraldo, have just had a daughter, Haley.

Big Youth—One of Jamaica's pioneering toasters, Big Youth was a rapping MC/DJ as early as 1970, years before the trend hit the U.S. His most recent album is entitled *Hia Luta Continua,* which is Portuguese for "The Struggle Continues."

Ruben Blades—The Panamanian-born singer and Harvard graduate has made nine groundbreaking solo albums which reflect his deeply felt social and political concerns. His latest album is *Escenas.*

Kurtis Blow—First established following the pop breakthrough of "The Breaks" in 1980, Kurtis Blow has consistently demonstrated his ability to communicate what the street community is thinking about at any given time. The title song of his most recent album, *America,* is a scathing indictment of the Reagan administration.

Bono—Bono, lead singer of the uniquely visionary Irish rock band U2—a band with a history of social concern and outspokenness—was so inspired by the "Sun City" project that he made an additional contribution just hours before the album was to be mastered. "Silver and Gold" is the result.

Duke Bootee—Rapper/songwriter Duke Bootee co-wrote "The Message"—one of the biggest-selling rap songs of all time—with Grandmaster Melle Mel.

Jackson Browne—Singer-songwriter Jackson Browne has been outspoken on a number of issues for many years. As one of the most highly respected people in the activist/musical community, he helped organize the 1979 "No Nukes" concert. More recently, he has appeared in a series of concerts promoting peace in Central America.

Ron Carter—Master bass player, composer, and bandleader, Ron is best known for his contribution to Miles Davis's classic recordings for Columbia Records throughout the 60s.

Clarence Clemons—The "Big Man" is the sax-blowing cornerstone of Bruce Springsteen's E Street Band. Clemons has also recently released his second solo album, *Hero.*

Jimmy Cliff—The legendary Jamaican singer and songwriter leaped to international stardom with the release of the movie "The Harder They Come" in 1972 and has continued to sing out for freedom and justice ever since.

George Clinton—His inspired musical marriage of James Brown and Jimi Hendrix broke down artificially imposed musical barriers twenty years ago. In addition to his own records, George has spoken through Parliament Funkadelic, Bootsy's Rubber Band, Ilfred Wesley & The Horny Horns, and, most recently, Fishbone.

Miles Davis—The legendary trumpeter, composer, and bandleader is nearly as widely respected for his lifelong defiance of American racism as he is for his immeasurable contributions to the music of the twentieth century.

Will Downing—An up-and-coming young singer, Will sang with Little Steven on the original demo of "Sun City" and remained on the finished version.

Bob Dylan—In the 60s Dylan awakened an entire generation to the unexplored possibilities in rock music by humanizing political and social concerns. His contributions to *this* generation include his roles on *We Are The World,* Live Aid, FarmAid, and now *Sun City.*

Fat Boys—This trio of teenage rappers is presently making a big splash via their starring roles in the movie *Krush Groove.* Their first self-titled LP went gold.

Fats Comet—Keith LeBlanc, Doug Wimbish, and Skip McDonald are Fats Comet. Originally, they were the innovative rhythm section of Sugarhill Gang, defining the sound of Hip Hop in the early 80s.

Peter Gabriel—A former member of the English band Genesis, Peter Gabriel has made several artfully conceived, ground-breaking albums and helped pioneer the fusion of African and Western music. He made his feelings on the subject of apartheid known with a song entitled "Biko," a tribute to the slain South African leader. His contribution to the *Sun City* album is his duet with violinist Shankar, entitled "No More Apartheid."

Peter Garrett—Peter is lead singer with Midnight Oil, a band whose songs have continuously addressed social and political concerns. In 1984 he ran for the national legislature in his native Australia on an anti-nuke platform and surprised a lot of people (not us) with the number of votes he received. Midnight Oil's most recent LP is *Red Sails in the Sunset.*

Bob Geldof—Lead singer of the Boomtown Rats, Bob helped make history this past year with his leadership on the Band Aid and Live Aid projects.

Daryl Hall and John Oates—One of the most successful duos in music history reached a new high when they introduced David Ruffin and Eddie Kendrick to a whole new generation at the Live Aid concert. Their tireless benefit work throughout the years, including the "Live at the Apollo" show, which donated profits to the United Negro College Fund, is well known.

Herbie Hancock—Pianist, composer, and bandleader Herbie Hancock had the biggest hit of his long and adventurous career (which included a lengthy stint with Miles Davis) with 1983's "Rockit," a song that integrated many different musical elements and revealed Hancock's virtuoso diversity. He is currently hosting the PBS show *Rock School.*

Nona Hendryx—Nona has devoted herself to thoughtful rock 'n' roll ever since the breakup of Labelle in 1978. Her own song about apartheid, "Rock This House," can be found on her latest album, *The Heat.*

Linton Kwesi Johnson—A political activist for black liberation from his youth, Britain's foremost reggae poet has published four volumes of poetry and released five LPs, his most recent being 1984's *Making History,* in which LKG tackles a variety of world concerns.

Stanley Jordan—Within the space of one year, Stanley went from playing guitar for loose change on the streets of New York City to his critically acclaimed debut at the 84 Kool Jazz Festival and Montreux Festival. Stanley's virtuosity in a variety of musical genres and his unique "two-handed tapping technique" have established him as a revolutionary guitar player. His self-titled debut LP was released this year.

Kashif—A romantic singer in the tradition of Marvin Gaye, Kashif has not only scored a series of hits on his own, he's also written and produced hits for George Benson and Whitney Houston. He's included an anti-apartheid song of his own composition entitled "Botha, Botha" on his latest album.

Eddie Kendrick and David Ruffin—They made history as members of the Temptations and have reunited for a new phase in their careers with a recently signed CBS record deal.

Little Steven—The writer and co-producer of *Sun City* first vaulted to prominence as guitarist and producer with Bruce Springsteen's E Street Band. Steven has led his own band, the Disciples of Soul, for the last three years. His most recent album, 1984's *Voice of America,* focused on Latin America, criticized U.S. foreign policy in the region, and called out for solidarity among the freedom fighters around the world and the people who already enjoy those fundamental freedoms.

Darlene Love—The star of many of Phil Spector's productions in the early 60s, Darlene sang lead on the Crystals' "He's a Rebel" and had a solo hit with "Wait 'Til My Bobby Gets Home." More recently, she starred in *Leader of the Pack*—the Broadway revue based on the songs of Ellie Greenwich—and has just signed with Columbia Records.

Malopoets—From Soweto, South Africa, the Malopoets perform what they call "township rock." Some of their members still live in South Africa, some are in exile. Their latest single is entitled "Song of the People."

Malopoets. *(Photo: David Seelig/Star File)*

Fat Boys. *(Photo: Reuven Kopitchinski)*

Grandmaster Melle Mel—One of the most respected rappers, Melle Mel got his reputation via a scathing series of message songs, including "The Message," "White Lines," and "New York, New York." His rap in "Let Me See Your ID" was the first to be recorded and it impressively set the pace for the rest of the record.

Michael Monroe—Lead singer and songwriter for the recently disbanded hard rock group Hanoi Rocks, Michael is currently working on his solo career.

Sonny Okosuns—A superstar bandleader and singer in his native Nigeria, Sonny Okosuns's songs often champion the cause of African liberation. One of the most notable is entitled "Fire in Soweto."

Bonnie Raitt—Equally at home with ballads, blues, and rock, singer Bonnie Raitt has for years been donating her talents to worthy causes, including the "No Nukes" concert at Madison Square Garden in September of 1979.

Joey Ramone—As lead singer of the Ramones, Joey helped kick off the mid-70s punk-rock revolution. One of the Ramones' most recent efforts was entitled "Bonzo Goes to Bitburg," which slammed President Reagan for equating the sorrows of the Nazis and the millions of Jews they slaughtered.

Lou Reed—Seminal New York songwriter and singer, Lou first came onto the scene in the mid-60s as a member of the Velvet Underground. His solo career these last fifteen years has been a model of quirky, intelligent, and uncompromising rock 'n' roll.

Keith Richards—As a founding member of the Rolling Stones, Richards helped introduce an entire generation of Americans to their own indigenous blues and rhythm-and-blues music. The Stones were also instrumental in sustaining and revitalizing the careers of the blues artists whose music originally inspired them.

Run-DMC—The most popular rappers in the world, due in part to such protest songs as "It's Like That" and "Hard Times," Run-DMC were the only rappers at Live Aid in July 1985. They currently star in the film *Krush Groove.*

Scorpio—An original member of the Grandmaster Flash and the Furious Five (he was known for a while as Mr.

Ness), Scorpio is just now embarking on a solo career. His first record is set for release in February of 1986.

Gil Scott-Heron—This political poet and singer made his debut in the early 70s, with "The Revolution Will Not Be Televised." He expressed his concern regarding the situation in South Africa as far back as 1975 with a song entitled "Johannesburg."

Shankar—The masterful electric violinist from India was first introduced to Western rock audiences via his 1970s association with guitarist John McLaughlin. He duets with Peter Gabriel on the "No More Apartheid" track on the *Sun City* album.

Bruce Springsteen—By way of highlighting the problems of the unemployed, the homeless, and the hungry, Springsteen contributed over a million dollars to community action projects in the cities he visited while on his 1985 "Born In the U.S.A." world tour. He also worked on *We Are the World* and "No Nukes."

Ringo Starr and Zak Starkey—Ringo's former band, The Beatles, are credited along with the Rolling Stones and The Who as having changed forever rock 'n' roll music and the youth-oriented culture that grew up with it. They also reintroduced millions of Americans to their musical roots. *Sun City* marks the first time the father and son drum team has ever played together on a record.

Tina B—Her song "Nothing's Gonna Come Easy" was one of the highlights of the *Beat Street* soundtrack. She and her partners in BLT (B.J. Nelson and Lottie Golden) also sang on the original demo of *Sun City.* She's currently recording her second solo LP.

Pete Townshend—The former visionary of The Who adds his distinctive guitar tracks to *Sun City.* Currently editing books and making films, Townshend resumed his musical career in late 1985 with *White City.* His reunion with The Who was a highlight of Live Aid.

Via Afrika—After two distinctive and innovative albums, *Via Afrika* and *Scent of Scandal,* these three female singers from Johannesburg showed up to perform on *Sun City* the day after they arrived in America as voluntary exiles.

Tony Williams—At age seventeen this nonpareil drummer was a permanent member of one of Miles Davis's greatest bands. At twenty-four he formed Lifetime with John McLaughlin and Jack Bruce, one of the first and most riproaring of the jazz-rock fusion bands. He continues to lead his own groups and to perform in a variety of idioms.

Peter Wolf—After thirteen albums as lead singer for the J. Geils Band, Peter Wolf stepped out on his own with *Lights Out!* in 1984. The J. Geils Band, along with Southside Johnny's Asbury Jukes and Bruce Springsteen, is credited with introducing in the 1970s traditional R&B combined with contemporary R&R to an audience that had never heard it before. He's currently recording a second solo album.

Bobby Womack—It took over twenty years, but Bobby Womack is finally becoming better known as the singer and songwriter of such smash hits as "I'll Still Be Looking Up to You" and "I Wish He Didn't Trust Me So Much" than as the writer for other singers of such classics as "It's All Over Now" (Rolling Stones) and "Lookin' for a Love" (J. Geils Band), as well as his own "Woman's Got to Have It." His influence has been widely felt throughout the music world and continues to be today.

Ron Wood—A member of the Rolling Stones since 1975, Ron was formerly the bass player with the Jeff Beck Group and guitarist with the Faces.

—Bill Adler

Stanley Jordan. *(Photo: David Seelig/Star File)*

"At Richards Bay, north of Durban, there are two beaches a few hundred yards apart. Alkantsrand, for whites, is equipped with nets to keep sharks away; Soekwater, for blacks, has no shark nets. Richards Bay is said to have one of the highest shark concentrations in the world."

The Apartheid Handbook, *Roger Omond, Penguin Books*

Segregation of beach facilities is but one manifestation of the injustices black South Africans face every day. A majority of the theaters, hotels, restaurants—even park benches—are segregated. *(Photo: The Africa Fund)*

Railways and buses are usually segregated as are most taxi services . . . . In 1984, a three-year-old Coloured boy, on a shopping trip with a white man, was refused admission to a 'whites only' taxi to take the pair home. The boy was left at the side of the road, twelve miles from home, while the white man went back alone. ''

The Apartheid Handbook, *Roger Omond, Penguin Books*

Forced to live outside the urban centers, black South Africans often travel great distances every day on crowded, segregated buses in order to get to work. In Pretoria, 71.3% of the 534,000 black commuters travel more than two hours a day, while 22.6% travel more than three hours to and from their workplace daily. *(Photo: Danny Schechter)*

(Opposite) Kashif and Nona Hendryx. *(Photo: David Seelig/Star File)*

L-r: Bruce Springsteen, Little Steven, John Davenport, and Zöe Yanakis. *(Photo: David Seelig/Star File))*

L-r: Miles Davis, Little Steven, and Arthur Baker. *(Photo: David Seelig/Star File)*

Vaal Reef Gold Mine, near Johannesburg. *(Photo: The Africa Fund)*

"The lyrics to 'Silver and Gold' are written from a prisoner's point of view, and it's set in a South African jail. Silver and gold are the reasons the whites colonized the blacks in South Africa. The song's about sanctions, which are very controversial. I've met with many people in Africa who've told me sanctions will hurt them and hurt them badly but that they're prepared to be hurt because that's the only thing that will get through to the people who are in control, because it's all down to Big Business —down to silver and gold."

—Bono (U2)

"SILVER AND GOLD"

words and music by Bono
© 1985 Solidarity Music

in a shit house, a shot gun
praying hands hold me down
if only the hunter was hunted
in this tin can town

no stars in the black night
look like the sky fall down
no sun in the daylight
looks like it's chained to the ground

broken back to the ceiling
broken nose to the floor
I scream at the silence
that crawls under the door

warden says, "exit is sold
if you want a way out . . ."
Silver and Gold
Silver and Gold

there's a rope around my neck
there's a trigger in your gun
Jesus say something
"I am someone"

seen the coming and the going
 the captains and the kings
 the navy blue uniforms
 them bright and shiny things

captains and kings in the slave ship hold
coins to collect . . .
Silver and Gold
Silver and Gold

the temperature is rising
the fever white hot
mister I ain't got nothing
but I've more than you got

chains no longer bind me
not the shackles at my feet
outside are the prisoners
inside the free—set them free

prize fighter in a corner is told
hit where it hurts
Silver and Gold
Silver and Gold

you can stop the world from turning 'round
you just got a pay, a penny in the pound

THE PROPAGANDA

"That black South Africans are materially better-off in economic terms than blacks elsewhere in Africa..."

THE FACTS

"...in terms of earnings per capita South African blacks are materially worse off than the citizens of at least 12 other countries in Africa— Kenya, Gabon, Nigeria, Ghana, Algeria, Libya, Tunisia, Niger, Cameroon, Ivory Coast, Zimbabwe and Botswana. The device through which Pretoria [the government] inflates the relevant statistics is to take the earnings of blacks in the predominantly industrial 'white-zoned' regions of South Africa, which though low are in some cases higher than in a number of other African states, as the representative sample and to present these averaged out, excluding the figures relating to many rural and Bantustan regions which it has declared 'foreign territory.' In this way it deducts the real poverty of most of South Africa's blacks, who are regarded as 'non-citizens.' The result is a grossly inflated image of black earnings. But if the real total of black South Africans is included in an economic analysis, South Africa scores far lower in black earnings than would be expected of a country with rich mineral resources, advanced agriculture and developed industries."

Apartheid—The Propaganda and the Reality
by Donald Woods

At Crossroads (where some jobs are available in nearby Cape Town), residents prefer the squalid conditions here — in 1983, between 5,000 to 10,000 people lived in the tent and shack camp—to the dire poverty and economic wasteland of the homelands. *(Photo: UPI/Bettman Newsphotos)*

CONSTRUCTIVE ENGAGEMENT

"'Constructive Engagement' [Reagan's policy of encouraging companies to maintain South African investments in order to promote reform] purports to persuade South Africa to dismantle apartheid. However, four years of 'constructive engagement' have seen an acceleration of forced removals of black communities from white-zoned areas, an intensification of penalties under the influx control regulations (trebling of fines and prison terms) and an escalation of the war in Namibia, as well as an increase in South African bullying of neighbouring states, with incursions and invasions into several of these states, and rising numbers of blacks killed by white soldiers and policemen in South Africa. Sharpeville has now been joined by Langa and Crossroads as symbols of ruthless repression. . . .Within four years of 'constructive engagement' Pretoria directly or indirectly caused the deaths of more blacks than in the previous 20 years."

Apartheid—the Propaganda and the Reality
by Donald Woods

The Johannesburg Stock Exchange: Black men keep track of the daily changes in white wealth. Constructive Engagement, as opposed to divestment, insures that white South Africans will continue to prosper. *(Photo: Danny Schechter)*

L-r: Kashif, Bono, and Nona Hendryx. *(Photo: Reuven Kopitchinski)*

Bruce Springsteen and David Ruffin. *(Photo: Reuven Kopitchinski)*

The track "Revolutionary Situation" was included on the *Sun City* album so that listeners could feel the urgency of South Africa's struggle.

The title was inspired by and features the voice of Louis Nel, South Africa's Deputy Interior Minister. In response to a boycott of classes by African children, he charged that they "were trying to bring about a revolutionary situation."

The voices, the screams, the gunshots are real—recorded in the streets, at rallies, and funerals in South Africa. The voices are those of ordinary people, and of such leaders as Nobel Prize winner Bishop Desmond Tutu and Nelson Mandela, the leader of the African National Congress who has been in prison for twenty years. Mandela's voice is intercut with that of his daughter, Zinzi, who is reading a letter from him to a freedom rally in South Africa. Since he is a "banned" person who cannot be quoted or interviewed, South Africans cannot hear his voice or read his words. Mandela's voice here is from a rare recorded interview in the early 1960s before his incarceration. The track also includes brief statements by South African State President P.W. Botha and President Ronald Reagan.

The song fragment threaded throughout the speeches is "Nkosi Sikelela Afrika," the outlawed national anthem of Black South Africa. "Amandla" is an African freedom cry. This track also features spontaneous rapping and music by Miles Davis, and the chanting of the Malopoets of Soweto, with percussion by Keith LeBlanc.

"Revolutionary Situation" was conceived, compiled, and edited by Keith LeBlanc and 'The News Dissector' in solidarity with the South African freedom movement. The audio is courtesy of International Defence and Aid in London and WBCN, Boston.

"Revolutionary Situation" was produced by Little Steven and Arthur Baker with Keith LeBlanc and 'The News Dissector' for the Sun City Record Project.

In South Africa, advocating divestment is a crime. In terms of the Internal Security Act (1982), advocacy of divestment or any other economic action against apartheid is punishable by up to twenty years in prison—whether the crime was committed inside the country or out.

South Africa Perspectives, *The Africa Fund*

"The argument is often made that the loss of foreign investment would hurt blacks the most. It would undoubtedly hurt blacks in the short run, because many of them would stand to lose their jobs. But it should be understood in Europe and North America that foreign investment supports the present economic system of injustice. . .We blacks are perfectly willing to suffer the consequences! We are quite accustomed to suffering." *Steve Biko, shortly before his death in 1977, while held in detention.*

South Africa: Questions & Answers on Divestment, *American Committee on Africa*

Bishop Desmond Tutu, Bishop of Johannesburg and 1984 Nobel Peace laureate, advocates divestment (...it is our last chance. It is a risk worth taking...) and continues to speak the truth, no matter what the possible punishment. *(Photo: Reuters/Bettman Newsphotos)*

THE FREEDOM CHARTER OF SOUTH AFRICA

The Freedom Charter *was unanimously adopted at a "Congress of the People," held in Kliptown, near Johannesburg, on 25 and 26 June, 1955.*

The Congress was convened by the African National Congress (ANC), together with the South African Indian Congress, the South African Coloured Peoples' Organization, and the Congress of Democrats (an organization of whites supporting the liberation movement). It was attended by 2,888 delegates from throughout South Africa, and was perhaps the most representative gathering ever held in the country.

The Charter was adopted by the four sponsoring organizations as their policy and became a manifesto of their struggle for freedom.

A year later, 156 leaders of these organizations were arrested and charged with "treason." They were acquitted after a trial lasting more than four years, but the ANC and the Congress of Democrats were soon banned, while the other two organizations were effectively prevented from legal operation by the banning of their leaders.

We, the people of South Africa, declare for all our country and the world to know:

— that South Africa belongs to all who live in it, black and white, and that no government can justly claim authority unless it is based on the will of all the people;

— that our people have been robbed of their birthright to land, liberty and peace by a form of government founded on injustice and inequality;

— that our country will never be prosperous or free until all our people live in brotherhood, enjoying equal rights and opportunities;

— that only a democratic state, based on the will of all the people, can secure to all their birthright without distinction of colour, race, sex or belief;

And therefore, we the people of South Africa, black and white together—equals, countrymen and brothers—adopt this Freedom Charter. And we pledge ourselves to strive together, sparing neither strength nor courage, until the democratic changes set out here have been won.

The people shall govern!

Every man and woman shall have the right to vote for and to stand as a candidate for all bodies which make laws;

All people shall be entitled to take part in the administration of the country;

The rights of the people shall be the same, regardless of race, colour or sex;

All bodies of minority rule, advisory boards, councils and authorities shall be replaced by democratic organs of self-government.

All national groups shall have equal rights!

There shall be equal status in the bodies of state, in the courts and in the schools for all national groups and races;

All people shall have equal right to use their own languages, and to develop their own folk culture and customs;

All national groups shall be protected by law against insults to their race and national pride;

The preaching and practice of national, race or colour discrimination and contempt shall be a punishable crime;

The people shall share in the country's wealth!

All apartheid laws and practices shall be set aside.

The people shall share in the country's wealth!

The national wealth of our country, the heritage of all South Africans, shall be restored to the people;

The mineral wealth beneath the soil, the banks and monopoly industry shall be transferred to the ownership of the people as a whole;

All other industry and trade shall be controlled to assist the well-being of the people;

All people shall have equal rights to trade where they choose, to manufacture and to enter all trades, crafts and professions.

The land shall be shared among those who work it!

Restrictions of land ownership on a racial basis shall be ended, and all the land redivided amongst those who work it, to banish famine and land hunger;

The state shall help the peasants with implements, seed, tractors and dams to save the soil and assist the tillers;

Freedom of movement shall be guaranteed to all who work on the land;

All shall have the right to occupy land wherever they choose;

People shall not be robbed of their cattle, and forced labour and farm prisons shall be abolished.

All shall be equal before the law!

No one shall be imprisoned, deported or restricted without a fair trial;

No one shall be condemned by the order of any government official;

The courts shall be representative of all the people;

Imprisonment shall be only for serious crimes against the people, and shall aim at re-education, not vengeance;

The police force and army shall be open to all on an equal basis and shall be the helpers and protectors of the people;

All laws which discriminate on grounds of race, colour or belief shall be repealed.

All shall enjoy equal human rights!

The law shall guarantee to all their rights to speak, to organise, to meet together, to punish, to preach, to worship and to educate their children;

The privacy of the house from police raids shall be protected by law;

All shall be free to travel without restriction from countryside to town, from province to province and from South Africa abroad;

Pass Laws, permits, and all other laws restricting these freedoms, shall be abolished.

The law shall guarantee to all their rights to speak, to organise, to meet together, to publish, to preach, to worship and to educate their children;

There shall be work and security!

All who work shall be free to form unions, to elect their officers and to make wage agreements with their employers;

The state shall recognise the rights and duty of all to work, and to draw full unemployment benefits;

Men and women of all races shall receive equal pay for equal work;

There shall be a forty-hour working week, a national minimum wage, paid annual leave, and sick leave for all workers, and maternity leave on full pay for all working mothers;

Miners, domestic workers, farm workers, and civil servants shall have the same rights as all others who work;

Child labour, compound labour, the tot system and contract labour shall be abolished.

The doors of learning and of culture shall be opened!

The government shall discover, develop and encourage national talent for the enhancement of our cultural life;

All the cultural treasures of mankind shall be open to all, by free exchange of books, ideas and contact with other lands;

The aim of education shall be to teach the youth to love their people and their culture, to honour human brotherhood, liberty and peace;

Education shall be free, compulsory, universal and equal for all children;

Higher education and technical training shall be opened to all by means of state allowances and scholarships awarded on the basis of merit;

Adult illiteracy shall be ended by a mass state education plan;

Teachers shall have all the rights of other citizens;

The colour bar in cultural life, in sport and in education shall be abolished.

There shall be houses, security and comfort!

All people shall have the rights to live where they choose, to be decently housed, and to bring up their families in comfort, and security;

Unused housing space shall be made available to the people;

Rent and prices shall be lowered, food plentiful and no one shall go hungry;

A preventive health scheme shall be run by the state;

Free medical care and hospitalisation shall be provided for all, with special care for mothers and young children;

Slums shall be demolished, and new suburbs built where all have transport, roads, lighting, playing fields, créches and social centres;

The aged, the orphans, the disabled and the sick shall be cared for by the state;

Rest, leisure and recreation shall be the right of all;

Fenced locations and ghettoes shall be abolished, and laws which break up families shall be repealed;

South Africa shall be a fully independent state, which respects the rights and sovereignty of nations:

There shall be peace and friendship!

South Africa shall strive to maintain world peace and the settlement of all international disputes by negotiation—not war;

Peace and friendship amongst all our people shall be secured by upholding the equal rights, opportunities and status of all;

The people of the protectorates—Basutoland, Bechuanaland and Swaziland—shall be free to decide for themselves their own future;

The rights of all the peoples of Africa to independence and self-government shall be recognised, and shall be the basis of close cooperation;

Let all who love their people and their country now say, as we say here:

"These freedoms we will fight for, side by side, throughout our lives, until we have won our liberty."

L-r: Rick Dutka, Owen Epstein, Arthur Baker, Little Steven, Bruce Lundvall, President of Manhattan Records, Ambassador Serge Elie Charles, Acting Chairman of the Special Committee Against Apartheid, and Igbal Akhund, Assistant to the Secretary General of the United Nations. *(Photo: David Seelig/Star File)*

THE UNITED NATIONS CENTRE AGAINST APARTHEID

"The Case for the Cultural Boycott of South Africa"

The following is excerpted from a speech made in May 1985 by H.E. Mr. Joseph N. Garba of Nigeria, Chairman of the Special Committee Against Apartheid, of the United Nations Center Against Apartheid. The occasion was a ceremony honoring Stevie Wonder.

. . . . I should like to take this occasion to explain clearly and plainly the background and purpose of the cultural boycott and the actions the Special Committee is taking in pursuit thereof. . . .

It [the cultural boycott] was the natural reaction of the artistic community to the stringent regulations issued by the racist régime in 1968 with the aim of completely prohibiting multi-racial performances and audiences. The General Assembly of the United Nations adopted a resolution at the time requesting "all States and organizations to suspend cultural, educational, sports and other exchanges with the racist régime. . .in South Africa which practised *apartheid.*" Trade unions of musicians and actors and other groups took action to persuade their members not to perform in South Africa. Many playwrights refused to allow the staging of their plays in South Africa. A number of Governments also took action. . . .

Many organizations of artists and performers have voluntarily taken action to strengthen the cultural boycott of South Africa. . . . Many individuals and organizations in this country have taken the same position. . . . Phyllis Hyman put the whole matter in perspective when, in rejecting a tempting offer from South Africa, she said: "I have a moral commitment that supersedes money". . . .

The case of those performers who go to South Africa knowing that there is a cultural boycott and aware of what is going on in South Africa calls for some comment. I shall not speak to those who are unable to resist the lure of the large fees. We should let their own consciences speak to them. I should only say that the huge fees. . .are an indication of [South Africa's] anxiety to break the cultural boycott.

I want to address those who feel that culture and politics should not be mixed or, that by performing before mixed audiences, artists are somehow helping to undo *apartheid.*

It is true that in recent years the South African authorities have begun to go back on the very stringent segregation of cultural events and audiences which was decreed in 1965. They have tried in particular to make a showcase of places like Sun City in the bantustan of Bophuthatswana. But such spurious desegregation is an optical illusion, put on show in order to mislead and delude an increasingly impatient world opinion. . . .

Let us be clear in our minds that, if any changes have occurred in this sphere, it is only because the cultural isolation in which South Africa finds itself today has forced the régime to rethink its policies.

Nelson Mandela

Nelson Mandela was president of the African National Congress (ANC) and one of the leaders of Umkonto We Sizwe ("the spear of the nation") at the time of his arrest in 1962. On trial for sabotage, Mandela made a statement from the dock:

"The African National Congress was formed in 1912 to defend the rights of the African people. . . .until 1949. . .it adhered strictly to a constitutional struggle. . . .in the belief that African grievances could be settled through peaceful discussions. . . .

"In 1960. . .the shooting at Sharpeville. . .resulted in. . .a state of emergency and the declaration of the ANC as unlawful. . . .[The ANC] went underground. We believed it was our duty to preserve this organization. . . .we had to continue the fight. Anything else would have been abject surrender. Our problem was. . .how to continue the fight?. . .fifty years of nonviolence had brought the African people nothing but more and more repressive legislation, and fewer and fewer rights. . . .

"It must not be forgotten that by this time violence had, in fact, become a feature of the South African political scene. . . .in 1957 when the women of Zeerust were ordered to carry passes. . .in 1958 with the enforcement of cattle culling in Sekhukhuniland. . .in 1959 when the people of Cato Manor protested against pass raids. . .in 1960 when the Government attempted to impose Bantu Authorities in Pondoland. Thirty-nine Africans died in these disturbances. In 1961 there had been riots in Warmbaths. . . . Each disturbance pointed clearly to the inevitable growth among Africans of the belief that violence was the only way out—it shows that a Government which uses force to maintain its rule teaches the oppressed to use force to oppose it. . . .

"Umkhonto [We Sizwe] was formed in 1961. . . . Attacks on the economic lifelines of the country were to be linked with sabotage on Government buildings and other symbols of apartheid. . . strict instructions were given to Umkhonto's members that on no account were they to injure or kill people in planning or carrying out operations. . . .

"It is not true that the enfranchisement of all will result in racial domination. . . . The ANC has spent half a century fighting against racialism. When it triumphs it will not change that policy.

"During my lifetime I have dedicated myself to this struggle of the African people. I have fought against white domination, and I have fought against black domination. I have cherished the ideal of a democratic and free society in which all persons live together in harmony and with equal opportunities. It is an ideal which I hope to live for and to achieve. But if needs be, it is an ideal for which I am prepared to die."

Mandela was sentenced to life imprisonment. Although the law prevents his picture or anything he says from appearing in print, he remains to this day one of the most popular leaders of the South African majority.

United Nations

The United Nations Special Committee against *Apartheid*

expresses its great appreciation to

Artists United Against Apartheid

for *its* valuable contribution to the
international campaign for the elimination of *apartheid*
and the establishment of a non-racial and democratic society in South Africa

Chairman
SPECIAL COMMITTEE AGAINST *APARTHEID*

"...though the black South Africans' needs are great, they do not ask for our charity; though the black South Africans' suffering is horrifying, they do not ask for our pity.
All they ask is that we look at them and see them, because by seeing them we see ourselves. Their struggle is our struggle. Because their struggle is not against men—that is a temporary condition—their struggle is against a disease, a disease called racism and bigotry. And that is a disease that we are all confronted with every day of our lives, in every country of the world...
We must reach inside and find the strength to work together to stop it once and for all. Because only together can we overcome this disease..."

Steven Van Zandt at the United Nations
Special Committee Against Apartheid reception,
October 30, 1985

TODAY IN PRISON*

by Dennis Brutus

Today in prison
by tacit agreement
they will sing just one song:
Nkosi Sikelela†
slowly and solemnly
with suppressed passion
and pent up feeling:
the voices strong and steady
but with tears close and sharp
behind the eyes
and the mind ranging
wildly as a strayed bird
seeking some names to settle on
and deeds being done
and those that will do the much
that still needs to be done.

*South Africa Freedom Day, June 26, 1967

†"Nkosi Sikelela Afrika" is the banned anthem of
 Black South Africa

119

GLOSSARY

African National Congress (ANC)—South African liberation movement founded in 1912 to struggle for a free and just South Africa. Banned by the government and forced underground in 1961.

Afrikaans—A dialect of the Dutch language spoken by Afrikaners in South Africa.

Afrikaners—White South Africans of Dutch descent who established the apartheid system. Afrikaners make up 60 percent of the white population.

Apartheid—South Africa's system of legalized racism. Apartheid denies all civil and human rights to the black majority and ensures the supremacy of whites.

Banning—A form of house arrest by which the government silences its critics. Banned individuals cannot be published or quoted, and their movements are restrained.

Bantustans—Name for barren wastelands making up only 13 percent of South Africa's land, which the South African government has declared the only place where Africans can live permanently.

Black Spot—Land in rural areas occupied by blacks, sometimes for generations, in "whites only" areas of South Africa. These communities are the first target of forced removals.

Black Township—The "blacks only" part of urban areas in South Africa. Townships are far from jobs, overcrowded with poor housing, little electricity or plumbing, and no sewage system.

Divestment—The withdrawal of funds from corporations and banks which support apartheid by doing business in or with South Africa.

Homeland—South African government's term for portions of land designated for blacks; bantustans.

Migrant Laborers—Those forced to leave their homes and families in rural bantustans to find employment in urban centers of "white" South Africa.

Namibia—(nah-MIB-ee-ah) The country which South Africa's military has occupied since 1915. Namibia was formerly called South West Africa.

National Party—The ruling party in South Africa led by the Afrikaners. It came to power in 1948 on a platform of white supremacy, legalized apartheid and stripped blacks of all rights.

Pan Africanist Congress (PAC)—South African liberation movement founded in 1959 based on black nationalism. Banned by the government in 1961.

Passbook—A document all blacks must carry at all times. Whites are not required to have one. Failure to carry a passbook results in arrest and jail for blacks.

Pass Laws/Influx Control Laws—Laws which control the movement of blacks. These laws forbid blacks to live in "white" areas and help the white government control workers.

Pretoria—The capital city of white South Africa. Also refers to the South African government.

Sharpeville Massacre—On March 21, 1960, the police shot and killed 69 blacks who were peacefully demonstrating against the pass laws.

South West Africa People's Organization (SWAPO)—The liberation movement fighting to free Namibia since 1966.

Soweto—A black township outside of Johannesburg. Over 2 million blacks live in this impoverished township.

Soweto Uprising—On June 16, 1976, South African police gunned down students in Soweto who were peacefully demonstrating against apartheid education. This began a series of protests and clashes with police around the country; over 600 people were killed.

From the South Africa Information Packet
The Washington Office on Africa Educational Fund

LITERATURE ON SOUTH AFRICA

The following organizations, which actively work to oppose the apartheid system in South Africa, offer a variety of literature which is available to the general public. Write or call for further details.

African National Congress (ANC)
801 Second Avenue, Suite 405
New York, NY 10017
(212) 490-3487

The American Committee on Africa/The Africa Fund
198 Broadway
New York, NY 10038
(212) 962-1210

American Friends Service Committee
Southern Africa Program
1501 Cherry Street
Philadelphia, PA 19102
(215) 241-7169

United Nations Centre Against Apartheid
United Nations Secretariat
New York, NY 10017
(212) 754-6674

International Defence and Aid Fund for Southern Africa
P.O. Box 17
Cambridge, MA 02138
(617) 491-8343

Namibia Concerns
Wartburg Theological Seminary
333 Wartburg Place
Dubuque, IA 52001
(319) 589-0328

National Council of Churches
Africa Office
475 Riverside Drive
New York, NY 10115
(212) 870-2511

Pan Africanist Congress of Azania (PAC)
211 East 43rd Street, Suite 703
New York, NY 10017
(212) 986-7378

South West African Peoples Organization (SWAPO)
801 Second Avenue, Suite 1401
New York, NY 10017
(212) 557-2450
(212) 986-7863

TransAfrica/Free South Africa Movement
545 8th Street S.E., Suite 200
Washington, D.C. 20003
(202) 547-2550

Washington Office on Africa
110 Maryland Avenue N.E.
Washington, D.C. 20002
(202) 546-7961

SUN CITY
ARTISTS UNITED AGAINST APARTHEID

AFRIKA BAMBAATAA · RAY BARRETTO · STIV BATOR · PAT BENATAR
BIG YOUTH · RUBEN BLADES · KURTIS BLOW · BONO · DUKE BOOTEE · JACKSON BROWNE · RON CARTER
CLARENCE CLEMONS · JIMMY CLIFF · GEORGE CLINTON · MILES DAVIS · WILL DOWNING · BOB DYLAN
THE FAT BOYS · PETER GABRIEL · PETER GARRETT · BOB GELDOF · DARYL HALL · HERBIE HANCOCK
NONA HENDRYX · LINTON KWESI JOHNSON · STANLEY JORDAN · KASHIF · EDDIE KENDRICK · LITTLE STEVEN
DARLENE LOVE · MALOPOETS · GRANDMASTER MELLE MEL · MICHAEL MONROE · JOHN OATES
SONNY OKOSUNS · BONNIE RAITT · JOEY RAMONE · LOU REED · KEITH RICHARDS · DAVID RUFFIN · RUN-DMC
SCORPIO · GIL SCOTT-HERON · SHANKAR · BRUCE SPRINGSTEEN · ZAK STARKEY · RINGO STARR
TINA B · PETE TOWNSHEND · VIA AFRIKA · TONY WILLIAMS · PETER WOLF
BOBBY WOMACK · RON WOOD

ALBUM AVAILABLE ON
MANHATTAN RECORDS AND HIGH QUALITY XDR CASSETTES